From Your Friends at **The MAILBOX**®

SCIENCE
IN A BOX
Grades 4–6

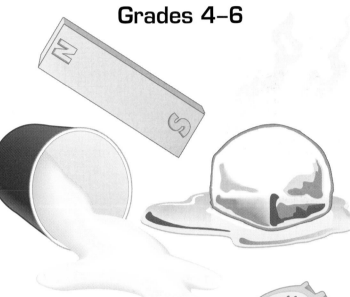

Table of Contents

More great science books from *The Mailbox*®:

TEC1731. Investigating Science—Animals • Grades 4–6

TEC1732. Investigating Science—Weather & Climate • Grades 4–6

TEC1734. Investigating Science—The Earth • Grades 4–6

TEC1735. Investigating Science—Space • Grades 4–6

TEC1737. Investigating Science—Light & Sound • Grades 4–6

TEC1738. Investigating Science—Energy, Magnetism, & Machines • Grades 4–6

SCIENCE IN A BOX

Writers: Bonnie Baumgras, Michelle Bauml, Diane Coffman, Terry Healy, Debi Kilmartin, Kimberly Minafo, Kathleen Scavone, Kelly Wade, Janice P. Wittstrom
Managing Editor: Cayce Guiliano
Contributing Editors: Denine T. Carter, Scott Lyons, Jennifer Munnerlyn, Deborah G. Swider
Copy Editors: Sylvan Allen, Gina Farago, Karen Brewer Grossman, Karen L. Huffman, Amy Kirtley-Hill, Debbie Shoffner
Cover Artists: Nick Greenwood, Clevell Harris
Art Coordinator: Nick Greenwood
Artists: Pam Crane, Theresa Lewis Goode, Nick Greenwood, Clevell Harris, Clint Moore, Greg D. Rieves, Rebecca Saunders, Barry Slate, Donna K. Teal
Typesetters: Lynette Dickerson, Mark Rainey

President, The Mailbox Book Company™: Joseph C. Bucci
Director of Book Planning and Development: Chris Poindexter
Book Development Managers: Stephen Levy, Elizabeth H. Lindsay, Thad McLaurin, Susan Walker
Curriculum Director: Karen P. Shelton
Traffic Manager: Lisa K. Pitts
Librarian: Dorothy C. McKinney
Editorial and Freelance Management: Karen A. Brudnak
Editorial Training: Irving P. Crump
Editorial Assistants: Terrie Head, Hope Rodgers, Jan E. Witcher

www.themailbox.com

What is *Science in a Box*?

Science in a Box is a collection of 39 quick- and easy-to-implement science units; each one fits into a shoebox for easy storage. Each hands-on investigation is designed to motivate students and encourage a love of science! These units can be used year after year with individual students, with small groups of students, as centers, or as class demonstrations. *Science in a Box* features 13 physical science units, 13 life science units, and 13 earth science units based on the National Science Education Standards.

Perfect for reinforcing content and process standards, each unit in *Science in a Box* contains the following:

- **The teacher page** features the unit's objective, a materials list, background information, an answer key for the student activity page, and fabulous facts.
- **The labels page** contains one challenger activity card and three color labels for the shoebox. The challenger activity can be used as an extension to the student activity, for students who finish early, or as a center.
- **The student activity reproducible page** is the main activity of the unit and features the purpose of the activity, step-by-step instructions, questions, and an explanation.

How do I assemble each box?

1. Cut out the three color labels located on the top half of the labels page. Glue the title label on one end of a shoebox. Glue the materials list and safety rules labels inside the lid.
2. Cut out the challenger activity card, located on the bottom half of the labels page. Laminate the card if desired; then place it in the shoebox.
3. Photocopy and laminate the student activity reproducible page; then place it in the shoebox. Or photocopy the page to make a class supply and place the copies in the box.
4. Gather the materials listed on the teacher page and add them to the shoebox. Read the teacher preparation section for any special instructions.

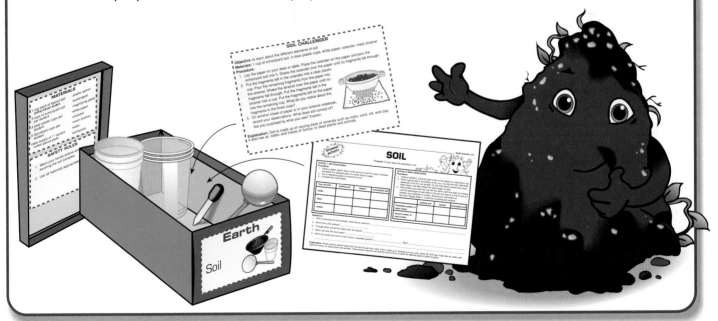

How do I know what objectives are covered?

The objective for each unit can be found on each teacher page. In addition, you'll find on page 160 an easy-to-use Objective Index listing the objectives for all 39 student activity pages as well as each challenger activity card.

MATTER

Convince your students that science does matter with this
Science in a Box *unit on the states of matter.*

Objective: to investigate the states of matter

Materials: resealable plastic bag, small wooden block, 2 plastic cups (different sizes), cornstarch, measuring spoons, class supply of small plastic cups, class supply of craft sticks, water

Teacher preparation:
1. Follow the directions on page 3 to assemble your *Science in a Box* unit.
2. Place the items from the materials list above inside the shoebox, except the water.
3. On the day of the activities, have water available for students.

Background Information

Matter is anything that takes up space and has mass. Matter can exist in the form of a solid, liquid, or gas. A *solid* has a definite shape and volume. The particles within a solid are tightly packed and little motion occurs. When a solid is heated, it becomes a *liquid.* The particles in a liquid move freely. As a result, a liquid does not have a definite shape. It takes the shape of its container. Its volume, however, remains the same when it is poured from one container to the next. When a liquid is heated, it becomes a *gas.* Gases have neither a definite shape nor volume. The particles in a gas may be far away from one another or close together. The volume and shape of a gas depend on the size and shape of its container.

Answer Key for Student Activity

Solid A. yes B. yes C. no D. yes
Liquid A. yes B. yes C. no D. no
Gas A. yes B. yes C. yes D. no
1. Matter is anything that takes up space and has mass.
2. Responses will vary. Accept all reasonable responses.

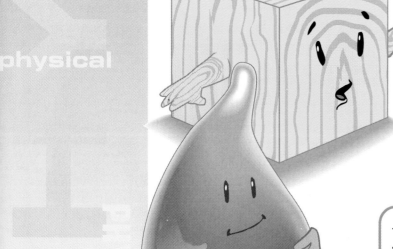

Fabulous Facts

The word *matter* is derived from the Latin word *mater,* which means "mother."

Gas particles move constantly and sometimes reach speeds of nearly 100 meters per second.

Not all solids keep a definite shape. *Amorphous* solids behave like slow-moving liquids. Candle wax, window glass, and tar are examples of amorphous solids.

PHYSICAL

Matter

©The Education Center, Inc.

MATERIALS

resealable plastic bag
small wooden block
2 plastic cups (different sizes)
cornstarch
measuring spoons
class supply of small plastic cups
class supply of craft sticks
water

SAFETY RULES

1. Do not drink the water in the plastic cups.

2. Do not eat or drink the cornstarch mixture.

MATTER CHALLENGER

Objective: to identify the state of matter of a mixture

Materials: 2 tablespoons cornstarch, 2 teaspoons water, small plastic cup, craft stick, measuring spoons

Procedure:

1. Measure the cornstarch and water and pour them into the cup. Stir the mixture with the craft stick. If necessary, add a small amount of water until the mixture is thick but can be stirred.

2. Tip the cup from side to side without spilling the mixture. On another sheet of paper or in your science notebook, explain whether you think the mixture is a solid, liquid, or gas. Describe the properties of the mixture to support your answer.

3. Pour some of the mixture into your hand. Try to roll the mixture into a ball. Observe what happens to the mixture. Record your observations.

Explanation: Certain *emulsions,* or fluid mixtures, become firm when stirred. The mixture has the properties of a solid when it is stirred and the properties of a liquid when left alone. These same properties can be observed when you walk along the beach. When your feet first touch the wet sand, it feels firm. When you stand for a minute the sand becomes more fluid, and your feet begin to sink.

©The Education Center, Inc. • *Science in a Box* • TEC1749

MATTER

Purpose: to identify the properties of matter in three states—solid, liquid, and gas

Procedure: Discover the properties of solids, liquids, and gases by completing the charts below.

Solid—wooden block   Yes/No

Hold the block in your hand.	A. Can you feel the mass of the block?	
Put the block in a cup.	B. Does the block take up space?	
Move the block to the second cup.	C. Does the *volume,* or amount of space the block takes up, change?	
Squeeze the block.	D. Does the block keep its shape?	

Liquid—water   Yes/No

Fill one cup half-full with water and hold it in your hand.	A. Can you feel the mass of the water?	
Observe the water in the cup.	B. Does the water take up space?	
Pour the water into the second cup.	C. Does the volume, or amount of space the water takes up, change?	
Tip the cup from side to side without spilling the water.	D. Does the water keep its shape?	

Gas—air   Yes/No

Blow air into the plastic bag and seal it. Hold it in your hand.	A. Can you feel the mass of the air?	
Observe the air in the bag.	B. Does the air take up space?	
Try to pour the air from the bag into a cup.	C. Does the volume, or amount of space the air takes up, change?	
Blow air into the bag and seal it. Squeeze the bag.	D. Does the air keep its shape?	

Questions:

1. Look at the completed charts. Notice which two properties all three states of matter have in common. Then complete the definition of matter. Matter is anything that _____

    _____

2. Think of a solid and a liquid that you use or see every day. Write them below. Then describe the properties of each one.

    solid _____

    liquid _____

Explanation: Matter is anything that takes up space and has mass. Matter can be found in three states: solid, liquid, and gas.

STATES OF WATER

Whet your students' thirst for knowledge with this Science in a Box *unit on the three states of water!*

Objective: to learn how water changes from one state to another through hands-on experiments

Materials: plastic container lid, small hair dryer, stopwatch, three 5 oz. reusable cups, ice cubes, water

Teacher preparation:
1. Follow the directions on page 3 to assemble your *Science in a Box* unit.
2. Label the three cups "cold," "warm," and "hot."
3. Place the cups and the items from the materials list above inside the shoebox, except the ice cubes and the water.
4. On the day of the student activity, have a supply of ice cubes available for students.
5. On the day of the challenger activity, have a supply of ice cubes and hot, warm, and cold water available for students.

Background Information

Matter can occur in three *states,* or forms: solid, liquid, and gas. The changing states of matter are *melting* (solid to liquid), *freezing* (liquid to solid), *evaporation* (liquid to gas), *condensation* (gas to liquid), *sublimation* (solid to gas), and *deposition* (gas to solid). Under appropriate conditions, each state can change into another. These transformations are called *physical changes.* During a physical change, the form of the substance changes, but the substance remains the same.

Answer Key for Student Activity

Observations:
melting—The ice becomes clearer and smaller as it melts. This process should take about one minute, 30 seconds.
evaporation—The amount of water slowly lessens until the lid is dry. This process should take about two minutes.
1. Melting is the change from a solid to a liquid.
2. Evaporation is the change from a liquid to a gas.

Fabulous Facts

Ice melts at 32°F (0°C).

When our body temperature rises, we sweat! As the sweat evaporates, it cools our bodies. Evaporation is a cooling process.

Dew results from the condensation of water vapor in the air.

Heat energy within the earth is great enough to melt rock. Lava is the liquid form of rock from deep within the earth.

Most matter expands when heated and contracts when cooled. Water, however, is an exception. When water becomes colder than 39°F, it expands!

PHYSICAL

States of Water

©The Education Center, Inc.

MATERIALS

plastic container lid   ice cubes

small hair dryer   water

stopwatch

marker

three 5 oz. reusable cups

SAFETY RULES

1. Use the hair dryer only as directed in the experiments.

2. Turn off the hair dryer after use.

3. Use hot tap water. Do not heat the water.

STATES OF WATER CHALLENGER

Objective: to observe the effects of heat energy on states of matter

Materials: three 5 oz. reusable cups, marker

Procedure:

1. Fill each cup halfway with the type of water labeled on the cup.
2. Place one ice cube in each cup.
3. Observe the ice cubes.

Questions:

1. In which cup did the ice cube melt fastest? Did you expect that result? Why or why not?
2. In which cup did the ice cube melt slowest? Did you expect that result? Why or why not?
3. What observations can you make about heat energy and changes of state?

Explanation: Molecules in hot substances move faster than molecules in cold substances. As the fast-moving molecules come into contact with slow-moving molecules, they transfer some of their energy to the slow molecules. This causes cold substances to become warmer. Therefore, the hot water will cause the ice cube to melt faster than the warm water and cold water.

©The Education Center, Inc. • *Science in a Box* • TEC1749

Note to the teacher: Use as directed on page 3.

STATES OF WATER

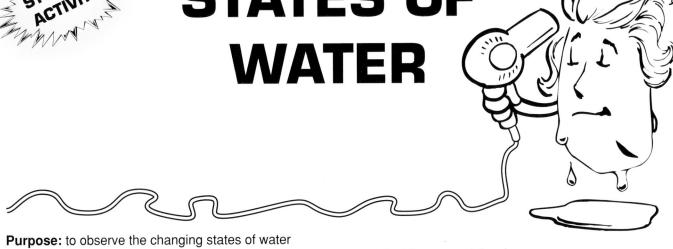

Purpose: to observe the changing states of water

Procedure: Use a hair dryer to change solid water (ice cube) into liquid water and then into water vapor.

1. Predict how long each change in state will take. Record you predictions in minutes on the chart below.
2. Place an ice cube in the lid.
3. Turn the hair dryer on to the warmest or highest setting. Aim the hair dryer at the ice cube and start the stopwatch.
4. Observe the ice cube. What changes do you notice?
5. When the ice cube is completely melted, stop the stopwatch and turn off the hair dryer.
6. Record your time and your observations on the chart.
7. Reset the stopwatch.
8. Turn on the hair dryer and aim it at the water in the lid. Start the stopwatch.
9. When the water has completely evaporated, stop the stopwatch and turn off the hair dryer.
10. Record your time and your observations on the chart.

Observation Chart

Physical Changes	Observations	Time	
		Predicted	**Actual**
Melting			
Evaporation			

Questions

1. Based on your observations of the changes in the ice cube, define *melting.* _____

_____

2. Based on your observations of the changes in the water, define *evaporation.* _____

_____

Explanation: Matter can change from state to state. For example, an ice cube (solid) can change into water (liquid), and water can change into vapor (gas).

FORCE AND MOTION

Put your science lesson in motion with this Science in a Box *unit on force and motion!*

Objective: to learn about force and motion with everyday objects

Materials: balloon, 2 paper cups, class supply of Fig Newtons cookies, quarter, 2 dimes, grooved ruler, marble, pencil, thick book, 3" x 5" index card

Teacher preparation:
1. Follow the directions on page 3 to assemble your *Science in a Box* unit.
2. Cut out a three-centimeter notch from the rim of one of the cups as shown on page 13.
3. Place the notched cup and the items from the materials list above inside the shoebox, except the book.
4. On the day of the challenger activity, provide students with the book.

Background Information

More than 300 years ago, an English mathematician, scientist, and astronomer named Sir Isaac Newton used three laws to explain how objects move. His first law of motion states that an object at rest remains at rest and an object in motion remains in the same motion unless acted upon by an outside force. The second law states that a change in an object's motion depends on the object's own mass and the strength of the force acting upon it. His third law of motion states that for every action there is an equal and opposite reaction.

Answer Key for Student Activity

1. Once the card is flicked away, the cookie drops to the bottom of the cup.
2. If the dime is flicked equally hard at both the quarter and the dime, the quarter won't move as far as the dime.
3. The balloon rockets into the air. A balloon with less air (less blown up) will not fly as far or as fast.

Fabulous Facts

Almost 300 years after Sir Isaac Newton's death, his ideas still affect our lives in many ways, from seat belts to space shuttles.

Edmond Halley, for whom Halley's Comet was named, encouraged Newton to publish his writings on gravitation and motion. Halley paid for their publication.

Sir Isaac Newton invented calculus, a type of higher mathematics.

PHYSICAL

Force and Motion

©The Education Center, Inc.

MATERIALS

balloon

2 paper cups

class supply of Fig
   Newtons cookies

quarter

2 dimes

grooved ruler

marble

pencil

thick book

3" x 5" index card

SAFETY RULES

1. Do not put a marble in your mouth,
   nose, or ear.

2. Use all materials appropriately.

FORCE AND MOTION CHALLENGER

Objective: to show how force applied to objects affects their motion and how motion is related
to the strength of the force applied

Materials: notched paper cup, grooved ruler, marble, pencil, thick book

Procedure:

1. Examine the illustrations. When the marble is released, will the height of the ruler make
   a difference in the movement of the cup? Record your predictions on another sheet of
   paper or in your science notebook.

2. To test your predictions, assemble each experiment and allow the marble to roll from the
   top of the ruler. Record the results.

Explanation: The higher the marble sits above the ground, the greater its energy. Thus the
marble hits the cup with greater force.

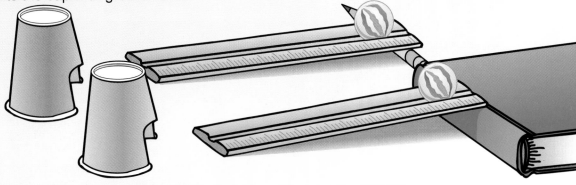

©The Education Center, Inc. • *Science in a Box* • TEC1749

FORCE AND MOTION

Purpose: to observe Newton's laws of motion with everyday objects

Procedure: Use the supplies in the box to set up each experiment shown below. Then follow the instructions below to conduct each experiment.

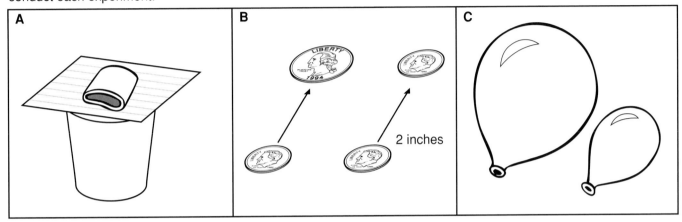

Instructions:

A 1. Predict what will happen to the cookie if you flick the edge of the index card, causing the card to fly out from under it. Record your prediction on the chart.
  2. Flick the index card from underneath the cookie. Record the result on the chart.
B 1. Predict what will happen to the quarter if you flick a dime at it. Then think what will happen to a dime if you flick another dime at it. Record your predictions on the chart.
  2. Flick the dime at the quarter. Then, with the same strength, flick the dime at the other dime. Record the results on the chart.
C 1. Predict what will happen if you blow up the balloon and then let go of it. Predict what will happen if you blow less air into the balloon and then let go of it. Record your predictions on the chart.
  2. Blow up the balloon and let it go. Then blow less air into the balloon and let it go. Record the results on the chart.

Predictions and observations:

A	**Prediction:**	
	Result:	
B	**Prediction:**	
	Result:	
C	**Prediction:**	
	Result:	

Explanation: (A) The cookie will remain at rest until acted upon by an outside force. Without the card under the cookie, gravity becomes the outside force acting upon the cookie. (B) The coins at rest are knocked into motion with the energy of the flicked dime. The distance they travel depends on the strength of the flick and their own mass. (C) As the air rushes from the balloon, an equal and opposite force acts on the balloon itself, rocketing it into the air. Less air in the balloon results in less force pushing against the balloon.

Note to the teacher: Use as directed on page 3.

INERTIA

Get your students moving with this fun Science in a Box
unit on inertia.

Objective: to learn about the law of inertia

Materials: clean, empty 20 oz. plastic bottle with the cap; golf ball; ruler; masking tape; small plastic cup; lima beans; paper towel; 9½" x 13½" gameboard or other sturdy board; 8 similar-sized books; water

Teacher preparation:
1. Follow the directions on page 3 to assemble your *Science in a Box* unit.
2. Place the items from the materials list above inside the shoebox, except the gameboard, books, and water.
3. On the day of the student activity, provide students with a folded gameboard or other sturdy board, eight books of similar size, and water.
4. Set up a ramp using two of the books and the board. Then measure one foot from the end of the ramp and mark a line (parallel to the end of the ramp) on the floor with masking tape. (See the illustration on page 19.)
5. Measure about three inches from the top of the ramp and mark a line with masking tape on the board.

Background Information

Sir Isaac Newton's first law of motion, also known as the law of inertia, states, in part, that objects at rest tend to remain at rest unless acted upon by an outside force. The force applied must be great enough to overcome this tendency to remain at rest or the object will not move. Scientists refer to this tendency to remain at rest as *inertia*.

Answer Key for Student Activity

Responses will vary. Possible responses:
Chart:
2 books—about 0"
4 books—about 0"
6 books—about ½"
8 books—about 1"
Questions:
1. The bottle moved the farthest when the ramp was eight books high.
2. The bottle will move farther as the ramp gets higher.
3. The bottle moves even though it is heavier than the golf ball because the golf ball gains speed as it rolls down the ramp. When it strikes the water bottle, it has enough force to make the bottle move.

Fabulous Facts

Better buckle up! If a car suddenly stops, an unrestrained person will continue traveling forward at the car's original speed until stopped by the steering wheel, dashboard, or windshield!

Super safety inventions like the airbag help reduce injuries in a crash by overcoming inertia and preventing a passenger from striking the interior of the car.

Inertia comes from the Latin word *iners,* which means "idle" or "unskilled."

PHYSICAL

Inertia

©The Education Center, Inc.

MATERIALS

clean, empty 20 oz. plastic bottle with the cap

golf ball   8 similar-sized books

ruler   water

masking tape

small plastic cup

lima beans

paper towel

9¹/₂" x 13¹/₂" gameboard

SAFETY RULES

1. Do not eat the beans used in this activity.
2. Use all materials appropriately.

INERTIA CHALLENGER

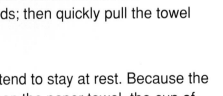

Objective: to observe an object remaining at rest as a result of inertia

Materials: small plastic cup, lima beans, paper towel

Procedure:
1. Fill the cup three-fourths full of lima beans.
2. Place the cup on the far left corner of the paper towel.
3. Predict what will happen to the cup of beans if you quickly pull the paper towel away. Write your prediction on another sheet of paper or in your science notebook.
4. Hold the opposite end of the paper towel with both hands; then quickly pull the towel away from the cup.
5. Was your prediction correct?

Explanation: According to the law of inertia, objects at rest tend to stay at rest. Because the cup of beans is at rest (not in motion) and has more mass than the paper towel, the cup of beans remains at rest when the paper towel is pulled. The cup's greater mass, and greater *inertia,* allows it to resist a change in state.

©The Education Center, Inc. • *Science in a Box* • TEC1749

Name _____

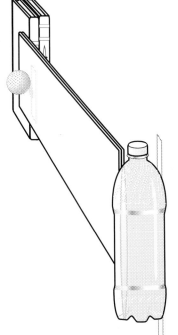

INERTIA

Purpose: to learn about the law of inertia

Procedure:
1. Fill the plastic bottle with water. Screw the lid onto the bottle, making sure it does not leak.
2. Place the bottle of water on the floor along the tape line as shown.
3. Predict how far the bottle will move when the golf ball is released from the top of the ramp.
4. Hold the golf ball on the ramp directly behind the tape line.
5. Release the ball, allowing it to roll down the ramp and strike the bottle.
6. Use a ruler to measure the distance the bottle moved from the tape line. Write your response on the chart below.
7. Repeat Steps 2–6 three more times—using four books, six books, and then eight books under the ramp.

Predictions and observations:

	Height of ramp			
	2 books	4 books	6 books	8 books
Prediction				
Result				

Number of inches bottle moved

Questions:

1. How high was the ramp when the bottle moved the farthest?

_____

2. What do you think will happen to the bottle if the ramp is raised higher?

_____

_____

3. Why do you think the bottle moves even though it is heavier than the golf ball?

_____

_____

Explanation: The ball has gravitational potential energy (GPE) because it is raised above the floor. The GPE increases as the height of the ramp increases. When released, the ball rolls down the ramp, converting its GPE into *kinetic energy,* or energy in motion. When the ball hits the bottle, it transfers this kinetic energy to the bottle. If it transfers enough energy, it will overcome the bottle's inertia and cause it to move.

©The Education Center, Inc. • *Science in a Box* • TEC1749 • Key p. 16

Note to the teacher: Use as directed on page 3.

REFLECTION

Shine some light on science with this
Science in a Box *unit on reflection!*

Objective: to learn about light reflection by observing reflections from various surfaces

Materials: mirror; waxed paper; aluminum foil; glossy magazine page; black construction paper; white construction paper; 8" x 10" piece of fabric; paperback book with a dark, glossy cover; shiny, dark ceramic mug; overhead transparency film

Teacher preparation:
1. Follow the directions on page 3 to assemble your *Science in a Box* unit.
2. Place the items from the materials list above inside the shoebox.

Background Information

The objects around us would not be visible without light. In ancient times, scientists believed that light was produced in the eye. Today we know that light comes from natural sources, such as the sun and other stars, and artificial sources, such as candles and flashlights. Other objects can be seen because light bounces off of these things and enters our eyes. This process is called *reflection.* When light from an image hits a smooth, shiny surface such as a mirror, the rays reflect in the same direction, and we see the original image. However, when light from an image hits a rough surface, the rays bounce off in many directions, and the image is not seen. Dark surfaces reflect images better than light surfaces.

Answer Key for Student Activity

no reflection—waxed paper, glossy magazine page, white paper, black paper, fabric
blurred reflection—shiny side of aluminum foil, ceramic mug, dull side of aluminum foil, paperback book cover
clear reflection—mirror
1. aluminum foil
2. They are all smooth and shiny.
3. paper plate; It has a rough surface and does not reflect an image.

Fabulous Facts

Scientists long ago thought the eye projected light onto its surroundings. Egyptian physicist Alhazen (965–1038) was one of the few scientists of his time to believe that light traveled from objects into the eye.

Italian artist Leonardo da Vinci was interested in the properties of light. He wrote many of his notes in mirror writing to keep them secret.

A *Pepper's ghost* is a large sheet of glass used on a stage that works as a window and a mirror. With proper lighting, the person at the side of the stage looks like a ghost to the audience and appears to walk through objects.

PHYSICAL
Reflection

©The Education Center, Inc.

MATERIALS

mirror
waxed paper
aluminum foil
glossy magazine
   page
black construction
   paper
white construction
   paper

8" x 10" piece of fabric
paperback book with
   a dark, glossy cover
shiny, dark ceramic
   mug
overhead transparency
   film

SAFETY RULES

1. Do not shine the light from the mirror into your eyes.

2. Use all materials appropriately.

REFLECTION CHALLENGER

Objective: to make a surface that reflects an image

Materials: black construction paper, white construction paper, overhead transparency film

Procedure:

1. Look closely at the white and black papers. Can you see your image? From which paper can you see more reflected light? Record your observations on another sheet of paper or in your science notebook.

2. Place the transparency film on top of the white paper. Examine this new surface to see whether it reflects an image. Record your observations.

3. Repeat Step 2 with the black paper. Record your observations.

4. At night, you cannot see your image when you stand outside and look straight ahead. But when you look through a window, you can see your reflection staring back at you. Use what you learned above to explain why.

Explanation: The smoother and darker the surface, the more likely we will see our reflection in it.

©The Education Center, Inc. • *Science in a Box* • TEC1749

REFLECTION

How can you see the objects all around you? You see things because light bounces from objects and enters your eyes. When you look at some objects, you can clearly see your *reflection,* or image. This is because all of the light rays reflect to you in the same direction. Other objects reflect light in many different directions, so you cannot see your reflection at all.

Purpose: to learn about light reflection by testing various surfaces

Procedure:

1. Use the Reflective Quality Code to predict how well the objects in the shoebox will produce a reflection. Record your predictions in the space provided.
2. To test your predictions, hold each object to your face. Look for a reflection of yourself or the things around you.
3. Use the code to rank the reflective quality of each object. Record the results in the space provided.

Reflective Quality Code

1 = no reflection			2 = blurred reflection	3 = clear reflection	
Object	**Prediction**	**Result**	**Object**	**Prediction**	**Result**
mirror			white paper		
waxed paper			black paper		
shiny side of aluminum foil			dull side of aluminum foil		
ceramic mug			fabric		
glossy magazine page			paperback book cover		

Questions:

1. Compare the surfaces of the construction paper and aluminum foil. Which surface is smoother? _____

_____

2. What do the surfaces of the items with blurred and clear reflections have in common? _____

_____

3. Which of the following materials probably reflects light rays in many different directions—a shiny silver spoon or a paper plate? Why? _____

_____

Explanation: All surfaces reflect light—we couldn't see them if they didn't. The surface of the material determines *how* that material reflects an image. Surfaces that are smooth and shiny produce a more accurate reflection than rough surfaces.

REFRACTION

Shed a little light on your science lesson with this
Science in a Box *unit on refraction!*

Objective: to learn about refraction and how it works

Materials: clear plastic cup, pencil, prism, crayons, water

Teacher preparation:
1. Follow the directions on page 3 to assemble your *Science in a Box* unit.
2. Place the items from the materials list above inside the shoebox, except the water.
3. The day of the student activity, students will need access to water.

Background Information

Light travels in straight lines at 186,282 miles per second through space. When light beams enter a transparent medium of a different density, they change speed and "bend" so that they appear to change direction. In water, this direction change appears to occur at the contact or boundary of the two different substances. The substances can be solids, liquids, or gases, but they must be transparent so that light can pass through them.

Answer Key for Student Activity

1. Figure 3
2. Figure 1
3. Responses will vary. One possible response: glass.

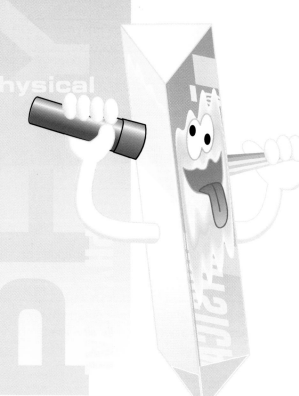

Fabulous Facts

A mirage, in which you seem to see water where there is none, is caused by light refracting in the atmosphere.

A rainbow is the result of sunlight (white light) refracting through raindrops. Sunlight is made up of many different colors, and when it passes through raindrops, each color bends at a different angle to form a rainbow band.

It takes about eight minutes for a beam of light to leave the sun and reach the earth.

Eyeglasses help people see better by refracting light in certain ways.

PHYSICAL

Refraction

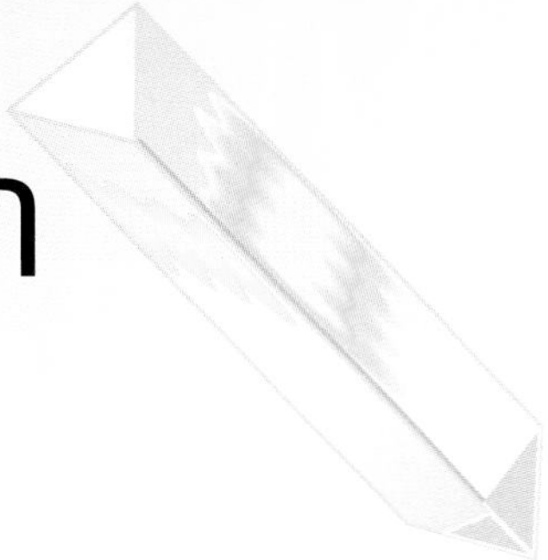

©The Education Center, Inc.

MATERIALS

clear plastic cup   crayons

pencil

water

prism

SAFETY RULES

1. Do not drink the water used in this experiment.

2. Be careful when handling a prism. Dropping it may cause it to break.

REFRACTION CHALLENGER

Objective: to learn about refraction through a prism

Materials: prism, crayons

Procedure: Hold the prism up to a light source such as a sunny window. Observe the refraction of the light as it passes through the prism. On a separate sheet of paper or in your science notebook, draw the diagram below. Color each section the color you see. Then explain why the light changes as it passes through the prism.

Explanation: As white light passes through a prism, different colors of light are bent by different amounts. The amount of refraction depends on a color's wavelength. Red light has the longest wavelength, so it is bent the least. Violet has the shortest wavelength, so it is bent the most. The other colors are bent according to their wavelengths, creating a rainbow of light.

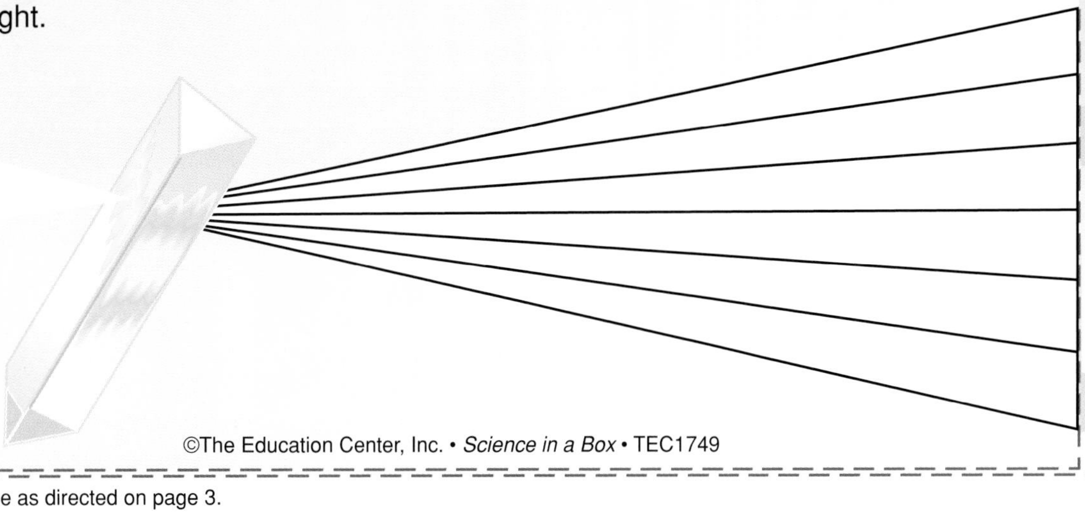

©The Education Center, Inc. • *Science in a Box* • TEC1749

REFRACTION

Purpose: to learn about refraction and how it works

Procedure: Fill the cup half full with water. Set it on a flat surface. Put the pencil in the water, holding it as shown in Figure 1. Observe the pencil by kneeling and looking at the pencil from the side. Hold the pencil at different angles as shown. Complete the drawings for each diagram. Then write your observations about how water refracts light on the lines provided.

Figure 1	Figure 2	Figure 3
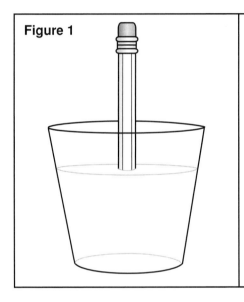		

_____ _____ _____

_____ _____ _____

_____ _____ _____

_____ _____ _____

Questions:

1. In which figure does the pencil (light) appear to bend the most? _____

2. In which figure does the pencil (light) appear not to bend? _____

3. Water is a good refractor of light. What other substance do you think would be a good refractor of light?

_____

Explanation: When light enters a clear substance of a different *density,* or thickness, it changes speed. This causes the light to appear to bend as shown by the pencil in the experiment. The greater the angle at which the light enters the substance, the greater the bending appears.

SOUND

Listen to the sounds of science with this Science in a Box
unit on sound!

Objective: to learn through a hands-on activity that sound is caused by vibrations

Materials: 3 small plastic cups, 3 metal brads, 3 craft sticks, two 16" lengths of cotton string, 24" length of fishing line, rubber band, plastic spoon, wooden spoon, metal spoon

Teacher preparation:
1. Follow the directions on page 3 to assemble your *Science in a Box* unit.
2. Use the tip of a pair of scissors or a nail to poke a small hole in the bottom of each plastic cup.
3. Cut the rubber band one time. Tie one end of the band to a metal brad and open the brad. Push the other end of the rubber band down inside the cup and insert it through the hole. Pull the band through the hole until the brad reaches the bottom of the cup. (The brad will anchor the rubber band inside the cup.) Tie the loose end of the rubber band to a craft stick.
4. Assemble another cup according to the directions in Step 3, using the cotton string in place of the rubber band. Then assemble the third cup, using the fishing line in place of the rubber band.
5. Place the assembled cups and the other items from the materials list above inside the shoebox.

Background Information

Sound is a form of energy that travels in waves. Sound causes molecules to push against each other, and as vibrations pass energy from one molecule to another, sound waves are produced. We hear sounds when vibrations reach our ears.

Fabulous Facts

Famous composer Ludwig van Beethoven composed music even after becoming deaf. He used the vibrations of piano strings traveling through a wooden stick to help him. Holding one end of the stick between his teeth, he placed the other end on the piano strings. The vibrations of the stick moved through his teeth, then through his skull, and finally reached his inner ears.

When you hold a seashell up to your ear, it sounds as if you can hear the ocean. Actually, it's the air inside the shell vibrating along with the sounds around you.

The loudest animal is the male howler monkey. It has two sound boxes, so when it howls, the sound can be heard three miles away!

Answer Key for Student Activity
1. The rubber band vibrated.
2. medium-low-pitched sounds
3. The sound was lower.
4. fishing line—high, rubber band—medium, string—low and soft
5. The sounds were different because of the different materials of varying lengths and widths that were used.
6. The sounds stopped when the vibrations stopped.

PHYSICAL

Sound

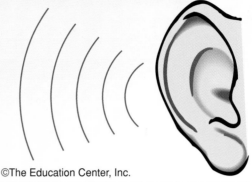

©The Education Center, Inc.

MATERIALS

3 small plastic cups
3 metal brads
3 craft sticks
two 16" lengths of cotton string
24" length of fishing line
rubber band
plastic spoon
wooden spoon
metal spoon

SAFETY RULES

1. In the student activity, pull the craft stick away from you in case the rubber band shoots out of the cup.

2. Never put objects into your ears.

SOUND CHALLENGER

Objective: to find out whether sound can travel through a solid
Materials: 16" cotton string, plastic spoon, wooden spoon, metal spoon
Procedure:

1. Tie the metal spoon handle to the center of the string.
2. Wind the ends of the string around your index fingers and place your fingers gently over your ear openings as shown in the illustration.
3. Lean over a desk or table so that the dangling spoon taps against it. What do you hear?
4. Remove your fingers from your ears and let the spoon tap the desk again. Do you notice a difference?
5. Predict what will happen when you repeat Steps 1–4 with the plastic spoon and then the wooden spoon.
6. Test your predictions.

Explanation: When you tap the spoon without having your fingers in your ears, the sound travels all over the room. Some of the sound waves reach your ears, so you hear a sound. With your fingers in your ears, the vibrations from the spoon travel directly up the string and into your ears. Sound travels better through a solid, like the string, than it does through the air.

©The Education Center, Inc. • *Science in a Box* • TEC1749

SOUND

STUDENT ACTIVITY

Purpose: to learn that sound is caused by vibrations

Procedure: Remove the three cups from the shoebox. Sit in a chair and place the cup with the rubber band attached to it between your knees. Pull the craft stick about 12 inches above the cup so the rubber band stretches. Pluck the rubber band with your finger and observe what happens. Then pluck the rubber band more gently and in different places. Answer the questions below.

Questions:

1. What did you see when you plucked the rubber band? _____

2. What did you hear when you plucked the rubber band? _____

3. What difference did you notice when you plucked the rubber band gently? _____

Predictions and observations:
On the back of this sheet, write your prediction for what you will see and hear when you try the experiment using the cup with the cotton string. Then predict what you will see and hear using the cup with the fishing line. Complete each experiment. Write what you actually saw and heard. Compare these observations to your predictions. Then answer the questions below.

Questions:

4. How were the sounds of the vibrating strings different? _____

5. Why do you think the sounds were different? _____

6. When did the sounds stop? _____

Explanation: Sounds are made when air vibrates. When the vibrations reach our ears, we hear sound. The size of the vibration and how fast an object vibrates affect the type of sound produced. In order for sound to be produced, there must be some matter for the vibrations to pass through. The only place where sound cannot be made is in space. That is why astronauts use radios to talk to each other in space. With no air to travel through, sound cannot be created.

Note to the teacher: Use as directed on page 3.

PITCH

Hit the high note with this Science in a Box
unit on pitch!

Objective: to learn about pitch through hands-on activities

Materials: plastic ruler, yardstick, 5 empty film canisters with lids, small paper clip, popcorn kernel, small pencil eraser, small piece of chalk, penny

Teacher preparation:
1. Follow the directions on page 3 to assemble your *Science in a Box* unit.
2. Put one item listed above in each film canister (except the ruler and yardstick). Secure the lid on each canister.
3. Place the ruler and the film canisters inside the shoebox.
4. On the day of the student activity, place a yardstick with the other supplies.

Background Information

Pitch is the degree of highness or lowness of a sound. Pitch is influenced by *frequency,* or the number of vibrations made by a vibrating object. When vibrations are close together, a high pitch is heard. When vibrations are far apart, a low pitch is heard.

Answer Key for Student Activity

Chart:
Observation responses may vary. Checked boxes for the ruler should show movement from high to low. Checked boxes for the yardstick should show movement from high or medium to low.
1. The pitch got lower.
2. The pitch got higher.

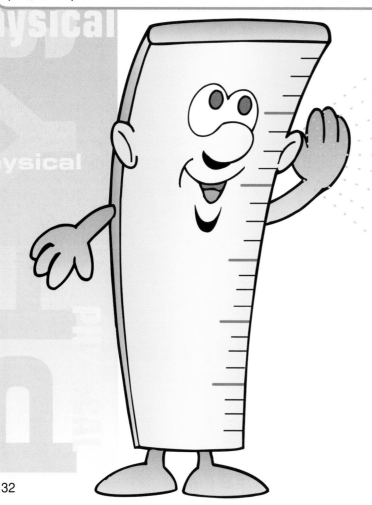

Fabulous Facts

Women typically have higher-sounding voices than men because their vocal cords are shorter. As a result, the vibrations of a woman's voice are faster, so the pitch is higher.

Bats, grasshoppers, and dolphins produce sounds that are over 100 times higher than the highest note a soprano singer can sing.

PHYSICAL

Pitch

MATERIALS

plastic ruler
yardstick
5 film canisters, each filled with a mystery
   item

SAFETY RULES

1. Make sure the top is secure before shaking each film canister.

2. Use all materials appropriately.

PITCH CHALLENGER

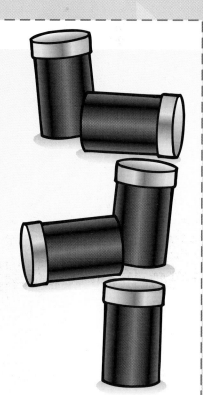

Objective: to identify levels of pitch
Materials: 5 film canisters, each filled with a mystery item

Procedure:
1. Shake each film canister, listening to the sound each one makes.
2. Listen to the highness and lowness of each sound. Arrange the canisters in order from highest to lowest pitch.
3. Open each canister and list the mystery items in order on a separate sheet of paper or in your science notebook. What do you notice about the level of pitch for each item?
4. Replace the top on each canister for the next group.

Explanation: An object's size, shape, and the material it's made from affect the level of pitch produced when it vibrates.

PITCH

Purpose: to learn about pitch

Procedure:

1. Place a plastic ruler on the edge of a table or desk. Position the ruler so that six inches hang over the edge of the desktop.
2. With one hand, hold the ruler firmly in place. With the other hand, pluck the end of the ruler three times.
3. Think about what you see and hear. Write your observations in the spaces provided.

    What I see: _____

    What I hear: _____

4. Predict whether the pitch you will hear will be high, medium, or low when you position the ruler at different lengths and pluck it. Record your predictions on the chart.
5. Test your predictions and record the results after each trial.
6. Repeat Steps 4–5 with the yardstick.

Predictions and observations:

		Ruler					Yardstick		
		Low	**Medium**	**High**			**Low**	**Medium**	**High**
2 inches	Prediction					**12 inches**	Prediction			
	Observation						Observation			
4 inches	Prediction					**16 inches**	Prediction			
	Observation						Observation			
6 inches	Prediction					**20 inches**	Prediction			
	Observation						Observation			
8 inches	Prediction					**24 inches**	Prediction			
	Observation						Observation			
10 inches	Prediction					**28 inches**	Prediction			
	Observation						Observation			

Questions:

1. What did you notice about the pitch as the amount of ruler or yardstick hanging off the table or desk increased?

    _____

2. What did you notice about the pitch as the amount of ruler or yardstick hanging off the table or desk decreased?

    _____

Explanation: When more of the ruler is extended over the edge of the desk, large, slow, deep-sounding vibrations are made as the ruler moves up and down. When less of the ruler is hanging over the edge of the desk, the vibrations are closer together and faster, producing a higher sound.

TRANSMITTING HEAT

Heat up your science class with this Science in a Box
unit on transmitting heat!

Objective: to learn about the predictable movement of heat

Materials: 2 quart-size, plastic, zippered bags; 2 thermometers; water-resistant marker; small plastic plate; warm water; cold water; small ice cubes

Teacher preparation:

1. Follow the directions on page 3 to assemble your *Science in a Box* unit.
2. Place the items from the materials list above inside the shoebox, except the water and ice cubes.
3. On the day of the student activity, provide students with very warm water and cold water.
4. On the day of the challenger activity, students will need access to small ice cubes.

Background Information

Heat transfer goes on around us and in us all the time. Heat moves or flows from hotter areas to cooler areas. This process of heat transfer continues until both areas have reached the same temperature. Heat is transferred by three main methods: conduction (through solids), convection (through liquids and gases), and radiation (through nothing at all).

Answer Key for Student Activity

1. The warm water should have become cooler, and the cold water should have become warmer.
2. The warm water transferred some of its heat energy to the cold water.
3. Responses may vary. One possible response: The cold water would have become warmer faster.

Fabulous Facts

Every 40 minutes the earth receives as much energy from the sun as all the people on earth use in one year.

Gabriel Fahrenheit invented the Fahrenheit thermometer. Anders Celsius was an astronomy professor in Sweden who invented the Celsius scale.

Even frozen objects have heat. An iceberg has more heat energy than a cup of boiling water. This is because the larger iceberg has many more moving molecules in it than the smaller cup of boiling water.

PHYSICAL
Transmitting Heat

©The Education Center, Inc.

MATERIALS

2 quart-size, plastic, zippered bags

water-resistant marker

2 thermometers

small plastic plate

warm water

cold water

small ice cubes

SAFETY RULES

1. Handle the very warm water carefully.

2. Do not drink the water used in the activity.

TRANSMITTING HEAT CHALLENGER

Objective: to find out whether an object's temperature will rise as its state changes

Materials: small plastic plate, thermometer, ice

Procedure:

1. Place the thermometer on the plate and the ice on the thermometer. Wait for the thermometer to adjust to the temperature of the ice. Then record the temperature of the ice on another sheet of paper or in your science notebook.

2. Predict what you think will happen to the temperature of the ice as it melts. Record your predictions.

3. Record the temperature of the ice every five minutes until it is completely melted.

4. Was your prediction correct?

Explanation: An object's temperature will usually rise when it is heated. However, in some cases heat causes the object's state to change before causing the temperature to rise. In the activity, the heat from the surrounding air causes the ice's state to change from a solid (ice) to a liquid (water) while the temperature stays the same. On another sheet of paper or in your science notebook, explain what you think will happen to the temperature of the melted ice if you leave the thermometer in the water for 20 minutes. After 20 minutes, check your prediction.

©The Education Center, Inc. • *Science in a Box* • TEC1749

TRANSMITTING HEAT

Purpose: to learn about the predictable movement of heat

Procedure: Remove the plastic, zippered bags and the thermometers from the box. Use the marker to label one bag "warm" and the other "cold." Next, partially fill the warm bag with very warm water and seal the bag. Partially fill the cold bag with cold water, add a few ice cubes, and seal the bag. Place the bags on top of the thermometers; then overlap the bags as shown. Record the temperature of each bag in the space provided below.

Prediction: What do you think will happen to the temperature of each bag of water? _____

_____

_____

_____

Observations	Warm Water	Cold Water
Starting temperature		
After 5 minutes		
After 10 minutes		
After 15 minutes		

Questions:

1. How did the temperature of each bag change? _____

_____

2. Why do you think the temperature of each bag changed as it did? _____

_____

3. What do you think would have happened to the temperatures of the bags if you had used hot water instead of warm water? _____

_____

Explanation: The atoms and molecules in all objects are constantly moving. In hot objects, the atoms and molecules move more rapidly than in cooler objects. If two objects are touching, heat energy always flows from the hotter object to the cooler object.

SIMPLE CIRCUITS

Energize your students with this Science in a Box *unit on simple circuits!*

Objective: to learn about simple circuits through hands-on manipulation of a lightbulb, a battery, and wires

Materials: AA battery, C battery, flashlight bulb, 2 pieces of insulated wire, rubber band, aluminum foil, tape

Teacher preparation:
1. Follow the directions on page 3 to assemble your *Science in a Box* unit.
2. Strip the ends of the wires.
3. Fold the aluminum foil into three strips.
4. Place the items from the materials list above inside the shoebox.

Background Information

In order for an *electrical circuit* to work, there has to be a complete path from the source of power (the battery), through the energy receiver (the lightbulb), and back to the source. Illustration A on page 43 is one example of an electrical circuit. The current flows from the battery through the wire to the lightbulb. Inside the bulb is a thin wire called the *filament.* The filament resists the electrical current. In doing so, the electricity heats the filament, causing it to glow. The current travels through the lightbulb and then back to the battery.

Answer Key for Student Activity

The bulb will light in A, C, F, and G.
1. no, yes, yes
2. The metal side of the bulb and the small metal tip on the bottom of the bulb need to be touched by the battery or wire.
3. The bottom of the battery (the negative end) and the small metal mound in the center of the top of the battery (the positive end) need to be touched by the bulb or the wire.

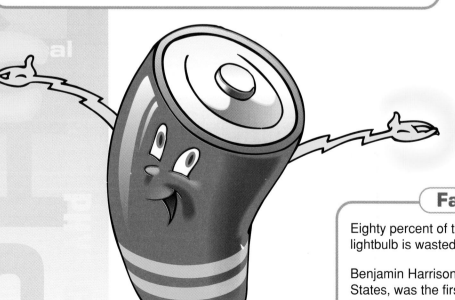

Fabulous Facts

Eighty percent of the energy used to light an ordinary lightbulb is wasted in heat.

Benjamin Harrison, the 23rd president of the United States, was the first president to use electricity in the White House.

The first battery was invented by Alessandro Volta (1745–1827), an Italian professor.

PHYSICAL

Simple Circuits

MATERIALS

AA battery

C battery

flashlight bulb

2 pieces of insulated wire

rubber band

3 pieces of aluminum foil

cellophane tape

SAFETY RULES

1. Never put a wire in a wall outlet.

2. Disconnect batteries when not in use.

3. Disconnect wires if they become warm.

SIMPLE CIRCUITS CHALLENGER

Objective: to make a simple circuit and short circuit

Materials: C battery, flashlight bulb, cellophane tape, aluminum foil (folded into 3 strips of "wire")

Procedure:

1. Examine the illustrations. Will the bulb light up in circuits A and B? Record your predictions on another sheet of paper or in your science notebook.

2. To test your predictions, assemble circuit A and then circuit B as shown. Hold the bulb in place.

Explanation: The electricity in circuit B never reaches the bulb. Instead, it takes a shortcut along the third strip of foil. On another sheet of paper or in your science notebook, explain in a brief paragraph why you think this arrangement is called a *short circuit*.

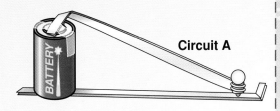

Circuit A

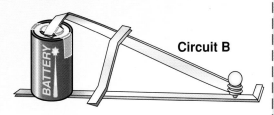

Circuit B

SIMPLE CIRCUITS

Purpose: to learn about simple circuits using a bulb, a battery, and wires
Procedure: Illustrated below are eight different ways to connect a battery and a bulb. Can you predict which four will make the bulb light up? Write your predictions in the correct spaces on the data sheet below. Then use the supplies in the box to create each illustrated setup. Record the results on the data sheet. (For C and D, use a rubber band to secure the wires as shown.)

| A | B | C | D |
| E | F | G | H |

Predictions and observations:

Data Sheet		
Will the bulb light? (yes or no)		
Letter	Prediction	Result
A		
B		
C		
D		
E		
F		
G		
H		

Questions:

1. Is it possible to make the bulb light by just touching it to the battery? _____
   Connecting it to the battery with one piece of wire? _____
   Connecting it to a battery with two pieces of wire? _____

2. For the bulb to light up, which places on the bulb need to be touched by the battery or wire?

   _____

   _____

3. For the bulb to light up, which places on the battery need to be touched by the bulb or wire?

   _____

   _____

Explanation: A bulb lights because electricity is flowing. The pathway the electricity follows is called a circuit. A circuit is a kind of loop. (The word *circuit* may make you think of the word *circle*. Does a circle have a beginning or end?)
   A battery is needed to make electricity flow. The drawing on the label of this box shows the whole circuit—through the wires, the bulb, and the battery. The arrow shows the direction in which the electricity flows.

PARALLEL AND SERIES CIRCUITS

Electrify your students' interest with this Science in a Box unit on parallel and series circuits!

Objective: to learn about parallel and series circuits through hands-on manipulation of bulbs, batteries, and wires

Materials: 2 D batteries, 2 rubber bands, 4 flashlight bulbs and holders, 9 pieces of insulated wire, aluminum foil, clothespin, tape, needlenose pliers, small Phillips screwdriver

Teacher preparation:
1. Follow the directions on page 3 to assemble your *Science in a Box* unit.
2. Strip the ends of the insulated wires.
3. Fold the aluminum foil into 2 strips.
4. Place the items from the materials list above inside the shoebox.

Background Information

With a *series circuit* or *parallel circuit,* more than one electric device may be powered by a single energy source. The electric current in a series circuit flows along one path. When the path is broken, electricity will not flow. In a parallel circuit, the current splits to flow along two or more paths. If one of the paths is broken, the electric current continues to flow along the other path.

Answer Key for Student Activity

yes; no
Observations:
series circuit—went out;
parallel circuit—remained lit
1. series; parallel; If one bulb burns out, the other two will stay lit.
2. All of the bulbs would go out.
3. parallel; When one light is turned off, the others stay lit.
4. Even if one bulb burns out, there's still a complete circuit with the other two bulbs.

Fabulous Facts

Long ago, train robbers learned that telegraph lines were wired in series circuits. During a robbery, they cut the line in one place to intercept the messages that were sent for help.

Some common series circuits include flashlights and tree lights. Household lights and appliances are wired in parallel circuits.

Almost all electric circuits are *complex,* which means they include both parallel and series circuits.

PHYSICAL

Parallel and Series Circuits

©The Education Center, Inc.

MATERIALS

2 D batteries
2 rubber bands
4 flashlight bulbs and holders
9 pieces of insulated wire
aluminum foil
clothespin

tape
needlenose
pliers
small Phillips
screwdriver

SAFETY RULES

1. Never put a wire in a wall outlet.

2. Disconnect the batteries when not in use.

3. Disconnect the wires if they become warm.

PARALLEL AND SERIES CIRCUITS CHALLENGER

Objective: to learn about parallel and series circuit setups for batteries

Materials: 2 D batteries, flashlight bulb, 2 pieces of aluminum foil (folded into strips), clothespin, tape

Procedure:

1. Examine the illustrations. Which circuit do you think will produce the brightest light? Record your prediction on another sheet of paper or in your science notebook.

2. To test your prediction, assemble each circuit as shown. Wrap the foil strip around the base of the bulb and then use a clothespin to hold the base, as it will get hot.

3. Record your observations.

Batteries in a parallel circuit

Batteries in a series circuit

Explanation: Battery power is measured in voltage. When batteries are connected in a series circuit, their voltage is added. For example, two 1.5-volt batteries will produce 3.0 volts. When batteries are connected in a parallel circuit, their voltage is not added, so two 1.5-volt batteries will still produce 1.5 volts.

©The Education Center, Inc. • *Science in a Box* • TEC1749

Note to the teacher: Use as directed on page 3.

PARALLEL AND SERIES CIRCUITS

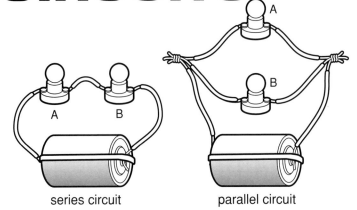

series circuit   parallel circuit

Purpose: to learn about parallel and series circuits using bulbs, batteries, and wires

On each circuit, trace the electrical path that includes the battery and lightbulb A.

In the series circuit, is lightbulb B included in the path you traced? _____ Is lightbulb B included in the parallel circuit? _____

Procedure:

1. Follow the pictures at the right to set up each circuit. Use the needlenose pliers to bend the wires as needed.
2. Unscrew lightbulb A in each circuit.
3. What happened to lightbulb B? Record your observations in the space below.

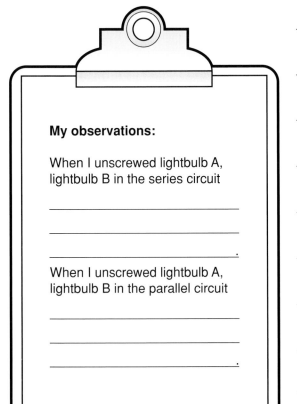

My observations:

When I unscrewed lightbulb A, lightbulb B in the series circuit

_____

_____

_____.

When I unscrewed lightbulb A, lightbulb B in the parallel circuit

_____

_____

_____.

Questions:

1. If you were setting up three lights in a model train station, which circuit would be easier to build? _____
   Which would be more practical and why?

   _____

   _____

2. Some strings of lights are wired in a series circuit. Explain what would happen if one bulb burned out. _____

   _____

3. Do you think the lights in your home are wired in a series circuit or a parallel circuit? Explain how you know. _____

   _____

   _____

4. On the back of this page, draw a diagram of a parallel circuit that contains three bulbs. Then, under your diagram, explain why you think the other bulbs will stay lit if one bulb goes out.

Explanation: In a series circuit, electricity must travel through one bulb and then the other. In a parallel circuit, electricity can travel along different paths at the same time.

ELECTROMAGNETS

Give your students a charge with this Science in a Box
unit on electromagnets!

Objective: to make an electromagnet with a battery, a nail, and a wire and to identify materials that can be magnetized

Materials: 2' piece of insulated wire; 2" nail; D battery; rubber band; clothespin; bar magnet; screwdriver; aluminum foil; pencil; large, straightened metal paper clip; box of small metal paper clips

Teacher preparation:
1. Follow the directions on page 3 to assemble your *Science in a Box* unit.
2. Strip the ends of the insulated wire.
3. Make a three-inch aluminum rod by twisting the aluminum foil.
4. Make a wire coil by wrapping the two-foot piece of wire around a pencil. Leave two inches of wire free at each end. Remove the pencil. Place the coil inside the shoebox.
5. Place the rubber band securely around the battery as shown on page 51.
6. Place the items from the materials list above inside the shoebox.

Background Information

Electricity and magnetism are closely related. Magnetism is a result of electric currents, and electric currents can be produced by changing magnetic fields. Just as electric charges attract and repel, magnetic poles also attract and repel. One important difference between magnetism and electricity is that the attraction between magnets is not affected by the material that separates them. The flow of an electric current, however, is influenced by the separating material and whether it is a good or bad conductor. An *electromagnet* is a temporary magnet made by running an electric current through a magnetic object. The illustration on page 51 shows an example of an electromagnet. The current travels from the battery through the wire and magnetizes the nail.

Answer Key for Student Activity

1. An electromagnet is called a temporary magnet because you can turn its magnetism on and off by stopping the flow of the electric current.
2. You need to be able to turn the magnetism off to release cars.

Fabulous Facts

In 1820, Hans Christian Oersted was the first person to show a connection between electricity and magnetism. While working with an electric circuit, he noticed that a magnetic compass needle moved when it was near the electric wire.

Telephones and doorbells have small electromagnets.

Electromagnets can be used to separate metal materials from other materials. Some electromagnets are powerful enough to lift a car.

PHYSICAL
Electromagnets

©The Education Center, Inc.

MATERIALS

2' piece of insulated wire

2" nail

D battery

rubber band

clothespin

bar magnet

screwdriver

aluminum foil

pencil

large, straightened metal paper clip

box of small metal paper clips

SAFETY RULES

1. Never put a wire in a wall outlet.
2. Disconnect batteries when not in use.
3. Don't touch charged nails or ends of wires.

ELECTROMAGNETS CHALLENGER

Objective: to determine which materials can be magnetized by electricity

Materials: coil of wire; small metal paper clip; D battery; rubber band; bar magnet; screwdriver; aluminum foil (twisted into a 3" rod); pencil; large, straightened metal paper clip

Procedure:

1. Test each object's magnetism (foil; screwdriver; large, straightened metal paper clip; and pencil) by placing it next to the bar magnet. Record your results on a separate sheet of paper or in your science notebook.
2. Connect the coil to the battery as shown.
3. Predict whether or not each object will become a magnet and attract the small paper clip when placed inside the coil. Record your predictions.
4. Place each object inside the wire coil. Test for magnetism by touching a small paper clip to each object. If the small paper clip "sticks" to the object, it is magnetic. Record your results.

Questions: What did the objects that attracted the small paper clip have in common? What other objects do you think could be used as electromagnets?

Explanation: Sending a current through a coil wrapped around a magnetic object turns the object into an *electromagnet,* or temporary magnet.

©The Education Center, Inc. • *Science in a Box* • TEC1749

ELECTROMAGNETS

You probably know about permanent magnets. They're the ones you find stuck to a refrigerator door. After completing this activity, you'll also know about electromagnets and why they're super magnets!

Purpose: to make an electromagnet with a battery, a nail, and a wire

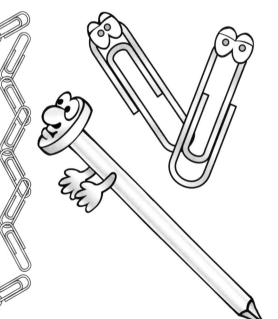

Procedure:

| **Step 1:** | Make an electromagnet. |

- Place the coil of wire around the nail.
- Leave one-half inch of the nail free at each end. Leave two inches of wire free at each end.
- Attach the wire to the battery as shown.
- **Caution:** Nail may be hot. Use a clothespin to hold the nail.

| **Step 2:** | How many paper clips do you think the electromagnet will attract? _____ |

Test your prediction and record the results. _____

| **Step 3:** | Predict what will happen to the paper clips if you break the circuit of the electromagnet by disconnecting one end of the wire from the battery. _____ |

Test your prediction and record the results. _____

| **Step 4:** | Remove the nail from the coil. Hold a paper clip back up to the nail. What happened? _____ |

_____

Questions:

1. Why is an electromagnet called a "temporary magnet"?

   _____

   _____

2. Why do you think electromagnets are better to use than regular magnets for picking up wrecked cars in a junkyard? _____

   _____

Explanation: When electricity flows through a wire, it creates a magnetic field around that wire. In electromagnets, unlike regular magnets, the magnetism can be turned on and off.

MAGNETIC POLES

Attract your students' attention with this Science in a Box
unit on magnetic poles!

Objective: to discover that all magnets have two poles and that like poles repel and unlike poles attract

Materials: disk magnet, 2 bar magnets with poles labeled, 3 ring magnets with center holes, paper clip, pencil

Teacher preparation:
1. Follow the directions on page 3 to assemble your *Science in a Box* unit.
2. Label the disk magnet by placing a small piece of masking tape on each side. Put one side close to the north pole of a bar magnet. If the magnets repel, label that side of the disk magnet "A." If the magnets attract, label that side of the disk magnet "B." Label the opposite side with the remaining letter. Place the magnets in the shoebox.
3. Place the paper clip, pencil, and remaining magnets inside the shoebox.

Background Information

The earth's magnetic poles exist near the North Pole and South Pole. Magnets also have north and south poles. If a bar magnet is suspended in air, it will rotate until one end points north and the other end points south. Magnetic force pulls opposite poles together (attraction) and pushes like poles apart (repulsion).

Answer Key for Student Activity

1. yes
   Data sheet: repel, attract, repel
2. Students' responses will vary but should include that opposite poles attract and like poles repel. My observation: The north side *repels* side A. The south side *attracts* side A.

   (N)   (S)
   side A   side B
3. Put the two like poles close together.

Fabulous Facts

The north magnetic pole is located in northern Canada, about 870 miles from the North Pole. The south magnetic pole is located in Antarctica, about 1,710 miles from the South Pole.

More than once throughout history, the magnetic north and south poles have switched positions.

The bodies of some animals, such as dolphins, have a magnet that acts as a compass and helps guide their way.

PHYSICAL

Magnetic Poles

©The Education Center, Inc.

MATERIALS

disk magnet   pencil

2 bar magnets with poles labeled

3 ring magnets with center holes

paper clip

SAFETY RULES

1. Keep magnets away from computers.

2. Do not throw or bang magnets together.

3. Never touch a magnet to a compass.

MAGNETIC POLES CHALLENGER

Objective: to examine the repelling power of magnets

Materials: 3 ring magnets (with holes in the centers), pencil

Procedure:

1. Slide two ring magnets onto the pencil. If the magnets stick together, pull one off, flip it over, and slip it on again.
2. Slide the third magnet onto the top of the pencil so that it doesn't stick to the magnet below it.
3. Push the magnets together; then let go and watch them spring apart.
4. Copy the picture shown on a separate sheet of paper or in your science notebook. Use what you have learned about like and unlike poles to label the remaining sides of the magnets, using "N" for north pole and "S" for south pole.

Questions: What makes the magnets spring apart? What do you think would happen if you removed the middle magnet and kept the top and bottom magnets in place? Record your prediction.

Explanation: Like poles repel and unlike poles attract. The three ring magnets will spring apart because like poles repel. When the middle ring is removed, the unlike poles of the top and bottom rings will attract each other.

©The Education Center, Inc. • *Science in a Box* • TEC1749

MAGNETIC POLES

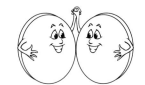

We usually think of magnets as being able to attract certain objects. But put two magnets together, and you'll discover that they sometimes do just the opposite.

Purpose: to discover that all magnets have two poles and that poles attract and repel

---

Pull Power

Every magnet has two *poles.* It is here that the magnet's force is strongest.

On a bar magnet, the poles are usually at the two ends.

On a disk magnet, the poles are usually on the two flat sides.

Question 1: Can both poles pick up a paper clip? Test your prediction.

Push Power

Sometimes two poles *attract,* or pull together. Sometimes they *repel,* or push apart. Predict what will happen when the poles of two bar magnets get close together as shown on the data sheet. Record your predictions in the space provided. Test your predictions by following the pictures to put the bar magnets together. Record the results in the space provided.

Data Sheet		
Will the magnets ATTRACT or REPEL?		
Magnetic Poles	**Prediction**	**Results**
S N N S		
N S N S		
N S S N		

Question 2: Write a rule explaining how magnetic poles behave when they are close together.

_____

_____

_____

_____

Name Those Poles

Put **side A** of the disk magnet close to the north side of the bar magnet.
Then put **side A** of the disk magnet close to the south side of the bar magnet.
Complete each sentence with "attracts" or "repels."

side A   side B

My observation: The north side _____ side A. The south side _____ side A.
Use your observations to label the magnet drawing. Write "N" for north and "S" for south.

Question 3: How can you make two magnets "push each other around"? _____

_____

Explanation: When two like poles are brought together, they repel, or push away. When two unlike poles are brought together, they attract.

PLANT AND ANIMAL CELLS

"Cell-ebrate" science with this Science in a Box *unit on plant and animal cells!*

Objective: to learn about plant and animal cells through hands-on activities

Materials: sand; glitter; glue; plastic wrap; scissors; red decorating gel; jar; 4 small bowls; nylon knee-high stocking; spoon; reference materials on cells; water; class supply of the following: 5" x 7" tagboard, small paper plates, marbles, 7 mm green pom-poms, 5 mm multicolor pom-poms, buttons, pipe cleaners, straws, rubber bands, pebbles

Teacher preparation:

1. Follow the directions on page 3 to assemble your *Science in a Box* unit.
2. Place the items from the materials list above inside the shoebox, except the reference materials, plastic wrap, jar, plates, bowls, and water.
3. On the day of the student activity, place the plates, plastic wrap, and reference materials with the shoebox.
4. On the day of the challenger activity, fill one bowl with sand, one with glitter, and one with pebbles. Place the jar and all four bowls with the shoebox. Have water available for students.

Background Information

All living things are made up of one or more *cells.* A cell is the basic unit of structure and function in an organism. Each cell's structure and content allow it to do a specialized job and contribute to the process of keeping the organism alive. Two important differences between plant cells and animal cells are that plant cells have *cell walls* and *chloroplasts;* animal cells do not. It is the cell wall that gives a plant its shape. Chloroplasts contain *chlorophyll,* which gives a plant its green color and helps the plant make its own food.

Answer Key for Student Activity

1. Responses will vary. Possible response: cytoplasm.
2. Responses will vary. Possible response: small pom-poms.
3. cell wall, chloroplasts; Responses to the second part will vary. Possible responses: tagboard, large green pom-poms.
4. The tagboard is firm and holds its shape like a cell wall.
5. Animals do not need to make their own food. They can hunt for food.

Fabulous Facts

Even though an ostrich egg can weigh up to two pounds, it is a single cell.

Nerve cells are the longest cells, sometimes extending several feet.

Prokaryotic bacteria are the smallest cells, measuring 0.2 micrometer.

The first living cells were described by Antonie van Leeuenhoek, a Dutch lens maker, in 1675.

Robert Hooke, an English scientist, first described a nonliving cell in 1665. The cell was from a slice of cork he observed under a microscope.

LIFE

Plant and Animal Cells

MATERIALS

sand
glitter
glue
plastic wrap
scissors
red decorating gel
jar
4 small bowls
nylon knee-high stocking
spoon
reference materials on cells
water

class supply of the following:
5" x 7" tagboard
small paper plates
marbles
7 mm green pom-poms
5 mm multicolor pom-poms
buttons
pipe cleaners
straws
rubber bands
pebbles

SAFETY RULES

1. Do not drink the water used in the activity.

2. Use all materials appropriately.

PLANT AND ANIMAL CELLS CHALLENGER

Objective: to learn about the cell membrane

Materials: jar; small bowl each of sand, glitter, pebbles; nylon knee-high stocking; rubber band; spoon; water; bowl

Procedure:

1. Put a spoonful each of sand, glitter, and pebbles into the jar. Add water until the sand is covered.

2. Stretch the stocking over the top of the jar and secure it with the rubber band as shown.

3. Gently shake the jar to mix the materials.

4. Hold the jar over the empty bowl and then carefully drain the water into the bowl.

5. Why do you think some materials pass through the stocking and others do not? In what ways do you think the stocking is like a cell membrane? Record your responses on another sheet of paper or in your science notebook.

Explanation: Cells create or absorb nutrients and release wastes. The cell membrane controls which materials enter and exit the cell. Explain how a cell membrane is similar to a colander or sieve.

Note to the teacher: Use as directed on page 3.

PLANT AND ANIMAL CELLS

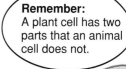

Remember: A plant cell has two parts that an animal cell does not.

Purpose: to learn the similarities and differences of plant and animal cells by creating a model of each

Procedure: Follow the steps below to complete the activity. Then answer the questions that follow.

Step 1: Research the parts of a plant cell and an animal cell.

Step 2: Create a plant cell and an animal cell model, using a piece of tagboard, two pieces of plastic wrap, a paper plate, red decorating gel, a pipe cleaner, large and small pom-poms, marbles, a straw, buttons, scissors, and glue.

Step 3: Using your models as guides, draw each cell in the space provided.

Step 4: For each cell, draw a line from each cell part to its name.

plant cell		animal cell
	cell wall	
	ribosome	
	cell membrane	
	mitochondrion	
	cytoplasm	
	vacuole	
	nucleus	
	chloroplast	
	endoplasmic reticulum	

Questions:

1. What does the plastic wrap represent on the plant cell?_____

2. The ribosomes are represented by what material on the animal cell? _____

3. Name the two parts of the plant cell that are not part of the animal cell. List the materials used to represent each one. _____

_____

4. Why is tagboard a good example of a cell wall? _____

_____

5. Plant cells contain chloroplasts. Why do you think animal cells do not? _____

_____

Explanation: Each cell has a specific job. The two cell parts found in plant cells but not in animal cells create two very important differences. A plant cell contains a *cell wall* and *chloroplasts.* The cell wall gives the plant its shape and support. The chloroplasts give the plant its green color and the ability to make its own food.

SYSTEMS

Get all of the parts of your classroom system working together with this Science in a Box *unit on systems!*

Objective: to learn that a system is a collection of parts working together to perform a function

Materials: flashlight with at least four removable parts, crayons, class supply of outline maps of North America, reference materials on North American biomes

Teacher preparation:
1. Follow the directions on page 3 to assemble your *Science in a Box* unit.
2. Place the items from the materials list above inside the shoebox, except the reference materials.
3. On the day of the challenger activity, have the reference materials available for students.

Background Information

In every aspect of our lives, systems are at work. Some, like the circulatory system, are examples of living structures working together to perform a task. Other systems, such as a simple circuit, contain nonliving parts that work together. Systems are only as good as the sum of their parts. If any part of a system isn't working properly, the entire system is at risk of breaking down. In living systems, this can mean the difference between life and death.

Answer Key for Student Activity

1. a. There would be no way for blood to be pumped.
   b. There would be no way for blood to move throughout the body.
2. a. There would be no place for inhaled air to go in the body.
   b. There would be no way for the lungs to expand.
3. a. There would be no place for digestion to begin.
   b. There would be no place for the digestive juices to mix with food.

Fabulous Facts

The first successful human heart transplant was performed by South African surgeon Dr. Christiaan Barnard in 1967.

The digestive system was studied by Dr. William Beaumont in 1822. Dr. Beaumont was able to closely watch the process of digestion by peering into a tube that was inserted into a wounded man's stomach.

A solar system consists of a star and planets or other heavenly bodies that orbit it. Even though our sun is approximately 93 million miles from Earth, both are part of the same large system.

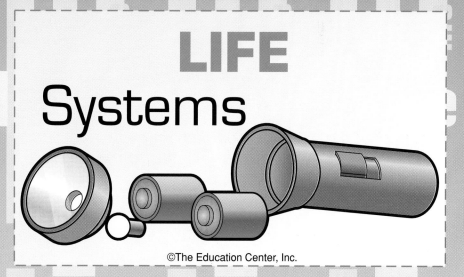

LIFE
Systems

©The Education Center, Inc.

MATERIALS

flashlight with at least four removable parts

crayons

class supply of outline maps of North America

reference materials on North American biomes

SAFETY RULES

1. Handle flashlight parts carefully.
2. Use all materials appropriately.

SYSTEMS CHALLENGER

Objective: to understand the impact of climatic systems on plant and animal life

Materials: class supply of outline maps of North America, crayons, reference materials on North American biomes

Procedure:
1. Use the reference materials to research the biome systems of North America.
2. Color each biome a different color on the outline map.
3. Using the chart to the right, write the average annual precipitation for each biome on the map.
4. On the back of your map, answer the following questions:
   a. Which biome gets the most rain?
   b. What types of plants and animals would you expect to live there?
   c. Which biome gets the least rain?
   d. What types of plants and animals would you expect to live there?
   e. What would happen to the plants and animals in a biome if the rainfall amount drastically changed?

Biome	Average Annual Precipitation
Tropical rain forests	100 inches
Deserts	4 inches
Grasslands	4–16 inches
Deciduous forests	30–100 inches
Taiga	8–24 inches
Tundra	10 inches

Explanation: Like other systems, a biome consists of interacting parts. Each biome has a different climate. The temperature, rainfall, and amount of sunlight all help determine the types of plants and animals that live in a biome. If one part of this system were changed, the entire system would be affected.

©The Education Center, Inc. • *Science in a Box* • TEC1749

Name _____

SYSTEMS

Purpose: to learn that a system is a collection of parts working together to perform a function

Procedure:

1. Take the flashlight apart.
2. List four parts of the flashlight on the chart below.
3. Reassemble the flashlight leaving one part out. Predict what will happen when the flashlight is turned on. Record your prediction.
4. Test the flashlight to see whether it works.
5. Write the results of your test in the space provided.
6. Repeat Steps 3–5 for each of the flashlight parts.

Predictions and observations:

Part	Prediction	Result

Questions: Think about how the flashlight requires all of the parts to work. Then consider each body system shown. On the back of this sheet, explain what would happen to the system if each part listed were removed and why.

1. Circulatory system
   a. heart
   b. blood vessels

2. Respiratory system
   a. lungs
   b. diaphragm

3. Digestive system
   a. mouth
   b. stomach

Explanation: A system functions because all of its parts are functioning. To be successful, most natural and man-made systems require that all of the parts work together correctly.

Note to the teacher: Use as directed on page 3.

ADAPTATIONS

Make your science lesson soar to new heights with this
Science in a Box *unit on adaptations!*

Objective: to learn how a bird's beak is an adaptation for the type of food it eats

Materials: tongue depressor, eyedropper, tweezers, pliers, scissors, sunflower seeds (in shell), 2 gummy fish, strip of beef jerky, 3 strips of Twizzlers Pull-n-Peel candy, cup of soil, small bowl, water, reference materials on birds

Teacher preparation:
1. Follow the directions on page 3 to assemble your *Science in a Box* unit.
2. Place the items from the materials list above inside the shoebox, except the reference materials, the bowl, and the water.
3. On the day of the challenger activity, place the two gummy fish in a bowl of water and the three strips of Twizzlers Pull-n-Peel candy in the cup of soil. Place the bowl, cup, and reference materials with the shoebox.

Background Information

Adaptation refers to the ability of living things to adjust to different conditions within their environments. A species must adapt to its environment in order to survive. Adaptations can take many generations or even millions of years to occur. One such adaptation is a *structural adaptation.* A structural adaptation involves some part of an animal's body. A bird's beak is an example of a structural adaptation. Beaks are tools used for obtaining and consuming foods.

Answer Key for Student Activity

Observations and results:
A. robin; sandpiper; tweezers; worms
B. hummingbird; eyedropper; water (nectar)
C. cardinal; hawfinch; pliers; seeds
D. spoonbill; pelican; tongue depressor; fish
E. hawk; owl; scissors; beef jerky

Questions:
1. It probably eats meat because its hooked beak looks like it would be useful in tearing.
2. Responses will vary. Possible response: They are both long, broad, and good for scooping.
3. Responses will vary. Possible response: chopsticks

Fabulous Facts

Keen eyesight helps the eagle find food on the ground from high in the sky. Just how keen is an eagle's eyesight? Some species can see a rabbit a mile away!

Roadrunners can run up to 23 mph to catch lizards and snakes for their meals!

An unusual skill of the dipper, a songbird, is that it can swim underwater for three minutes. This is helpful in finding fish eggs to eat.

LIFE

Adaptations

©The Education Center, Inc.

MATERIALS

tongue depressor

eyedropper

sunflower seeds
  (in shell)

2 gummy fish

strip of beef jerky

tweezers

pliers

scissors

3 strips of Twizzlers
  Pull-n-Peel candy

cup of soil

reference materials
  on birds

small bowl

water

SAFETY RULES

1. Do not eat any of the foods used in the activities.

2. Use all materials appropriately.

ADAPTATIONS CHALLENGER

Objective: to determine how a bird adapts its feeding strategy when its environment abruptly changes

Materials: tongue depressor, eyedropper, sunflower seeds, 2 gummy fish in a bowl of water, strip of beef jerky, tweezers, pliers, scissors, 3 strips of Twizzlers Pull-n-Peel candy in a cup of soil, reference materials on birds

Procedure:

1. Select a berry-eating bird from the reference materials. Research the bird's habitat and how it eats. On another sheet of paper or in your science notebook, write a summary of your findings and sketch a picture of your bird.

2. How might your bird's feeding habits adapt if its environment experienced an abrupt change? For example, what would a berry-eating bird do if all the berries disappeared? Select the beak model from the box that best represents your bird's beak (scissors, pliers, tweezers, eyedropper, or tongue depressor). Using the model, try to pick up the seeds, fish, beef jerky, worms, and nectar (water). Think about which food(s) your bird might be able to eat.

Explanation: An animal must be able to find food in its current habitat or move to another one in order to survive. Some animals can change their food source to one that is more readily available in their environment.

©The Education Center, Inc. • *Science in a Box* • TEC1749

Name _____

ADAPTATIONS

| hawfinch | northern cardinal | red-tailed hawk | ruby-throated hummingbird | roseate spoonbill |
| spotted sandpiper | barn owl | American robin | American white pelican | |

Purpose: to learn about bird beak adaptations using a variety of models

Procedure:
1. Study the bird pictures.
2. Read the bird beak descriptions in the chart below.
3. Look at the scissors, pliers, tweezers, eyedropper, and tongue depressor. Think about which item would best model each type of beak based on the bird pictures.
4. Try to pick up the water (nectar), fish, beef jerky (small mammal), seeds, and worms with each model to find out which one is best suited to pick up each food.
5. On the chart below, record the birds that have each type of beak, the beak model used, and the food that was easiest to pick up.

Observations and results:

Beak	Bird	Model	Food
A. pointed, probelike			
B. long, strawlike			
C. short, conelike			
D. long, large, scooplike			
E. hooked, short			

Questions:

1. Look at the owl's beak. What kind of food might it eat and why?

_____

2. What characteristics do the spoonbill's beak and the tongue depressor have in common?

_____

3. What other beak models could be used for the robin?

_____

Explanation:

All animals must adapt to their environments in order to survive. For a bird, its beak has been adapted for use as a tool to pick up and consume food. The shape of a bird's beak suggests what types of food it may eat.

Note to the teacher: Use as directed on page 3.

PLANT LIFE CYCLES

Turn a school day into a season of learning with this Science in a Box *unit on the life cycles of plants!*

Objective: to understand the life cycles of plants

Materials: hand lens; scissors; reference materials on plants; crayons or markers; glue; 3 pea seeds per student; class supply each of lima bean seeds, corn seeds, pea pods, small paper plates, toothpicks, light-colored construction paper

Teacher preparation:
1. Follow the directions on page 3 to assemble your *Science in a Box* unit.
2. Place the items from the materials list above inside the shoebox, except the reference materials.
3. The day before the student activity, soak the lima bean seeds and corn seeds in water overnight.
4. On the day of each activity, provide reference materials on plants for students.

Background Information

As living things, plants grow and reproduce. Green plants reproduce by making seeds. Each seed has all the basic parts needed to grow into a plant. It also has a food supply to use for energy until it can make its own. When the conditions are right, the seed *germinates,* or begins to grow. The seed's protective case breaks open; the root grows downward; and then a shoot, which will produce a stem and leaves, grows upward. As the shoot grows longer, it breaks through the soil's surface. As the leaves grow, they use sunlight to make food for the plant through a process called *photosynthesis.* Soon, a flower grows. The flower produces seeds. And the cycle begins again.

Answer Key for Student Activity

1. Both seeds have an embryo, a seed coat, a cotyledon, a root, and a shoot.
2. The lima bean seed has two cotyledons and a leaf. The corn seed has one cotyledon and an endosperm.
3. The corn seed is a monocot. The lima bean seed is a dicot. A corn seed is a monocot because it has one cotyledon. The lima bean seed is a dicot because it has two cotyledons.

Fabulous Facts

Seedlings, or small plants, can exert great force. Some plants can push through a newly tarred road!

The squirting cucumber shoots seeds up to 26$\frac{1}{2}$ feet away!

Some of the largest leaves in the world come from the raffia palm. They can be up to 65 feet long!

Frozen lupine seeds found in the Arctic are believed to be 10,000–15,000 years old. Once defrosted, some actually germinated!

A rare plant in the Andes does not flower until it is about 150 years old.

LIFE

Plant Life Cycles

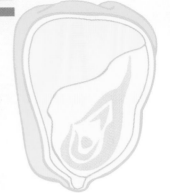

©The Education Center, Inc.

MATERIALS

hand lens
scissors
crayons or
　markers
glue
3 pea seeds
　per student
reference materials
　on plants

class supply each of
　lima bean seeds
　corn seeds
　pea pods
　toothpicks
　light-colored
　　construction
　　paper
　small paper plates

SAFETY RULES

1. Wash your hands before and after handling seeds.

2. Do not eat the seeds used in the activities.

3. Use all materials appropriately.

PLANT LIFE CYCLES CHALLENGER

Objective: to learn about the life cycle of a plant
Materials: reference materials on plants, pea pod,
3 pea seeds, crayons or markers, glue, light-colored
construction paper
Procedure:
1. Research the life cycle of a plant.
2. On a sheet of construction paper, draw the diagram shown.
3. Use three pea seeds, a pea pod, crayons or markers, and glue to create a diagram of the life cycle of a plant. Label each stage.
4. On another sheet of paper or in your science notebook, answer the following questions: What does the pea pod represent in the life cycle diagram? Why is a life cycle drawn as a circle? Could the cycle continue if one stage were missing?

Explanation: The life cycle of a plant is a continuous process. A plant sprouts from a seed, grows and matures, flowers, and produces seeds.

PLANT LIFE CYCLES

Purpose: to learn that seeds have the basic parts needed to grow into a plant

A *cotyledon,* or leaflike structure, absorbs and digests the food stored in a seed. Some seed plants are *monocots* and have seeds with only one cotyledon. Some are *dicots* and have seeds with two cotyledons.

Procedure:

1. Place a lima bean seed and a corn seed on a small paper plate.
2. Using a toothpick, carefully split open the lima bean seed. Using a pair of scissors, cut the corn seed in half.
3. Use the hand lens to look closely at the seeds.
4. Label the drawings with the names of the seed parts using the words in the word bank. Use reference materials if necessary. **Hint:** All words will be used. Some words will be used more than once.

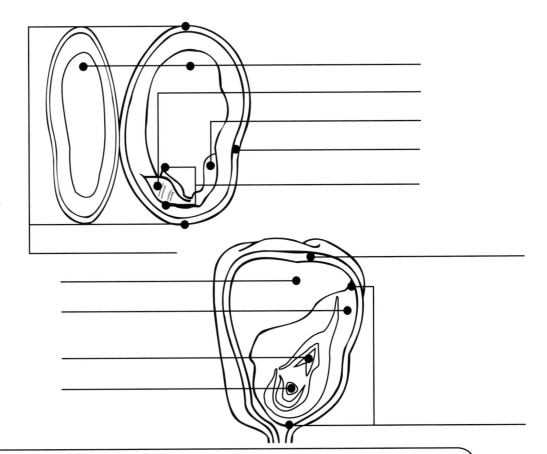

Word Bank: seed coat   cotyledon   endosperm   root   shoot   leaf   embryo

Questions:

1. What do the seeds have in common? _____

_____

2. What are the differences in the seeds? _____

_____

3. Which seed is a monocot? _____

   Which is a dicot? _____ How do you know? _____

_____

Explanation: There are different types of seeds, but all seeds contain the basic parts needed to grow into a plant.

©The Education Center, Inc. • *Science in a Box* • TEC1749 • Key p. 68

ANIMAL LIFE CYCLES

Get more life out of your science lesson with this Science in a Box *unit on animal life cycles!*

Objective: to learn about animal life cycles through hands-on activities

Materials: 4 sheets of 12" x 18" light-colored construction paper per student, class supply of 9" x 12" construction paper, tape, scissors, 5 different colors of yarn, markers or crayons, 2 metal brads per student, compass

Teacher preparation:
1. Follow the directions on page 3 to assemble your *Science in a Box* unit.
2. Place the items from the materials list above inside the shoebox, except the 12" x 18" paper.
3. On the day of the student activity, have two sheets of 12" x 18" construction paper available for each student.
4. On the day of the challenger activity, have two sheets of 12" x 18" construction paper available for each student.

Background Information

Most organisms go through stages of life. These stages make up an organism's *life cycle*. A human's life cycle consists of infancy, childhood, adolescence, and adulthood. An insect with a complete metamorphosis goes through four stages: egg, larva, pupa, and adult.

Answer Key for Student Activity

Responses will vary. Accept all reasonable responses.

Fabulous Facts

A mayfly's life cycle is completed in a few hours.

One animal with a long *gestation period,* or time it takes a baby to develop in the mother, is the Indian elephant. The baby takes almost two years to develop before birth.

At birth, a blue whale can weigh up to seven tons.

A nest made of foam? That's right! The gray tree frog builds a nest of foam hanging over water, and as the tadpoles hatch, they drop through the foam.

LIFE

Animal Life Cycles

©The Education Center, Inc.

MATERIALS

tape
scissors
compass
4 sheets of 12" x 18" light-colored construction
   paper per student
class supply of 9" x 12" construction paper

markers or crayons
5 different colors of yarn
2 metal brads per student

SAFETY RULES

1. Use all materials appropriately.

2. Be careful when using a metal brad to poke a hole through paper.

ANIMAL LIFE CYCLES CHALLENGER

Objective: to learn about three factors in an animal's life cycle

Materials: 2 sheets of 12" x 18" construction paper, sheet of 9" x 12" construction paper, 5 different colors of yarn, tape, scissors

Procedure: Choose one color of yarn to represent each animal. Then use the information from the chart (Fig. 1) and the directions below to make three graphs.

1. On one large sheet of construction paper, copy the graph (Fig. 2). Label the vertical axis "1 cm = 1 year." Then measure 1 cm of string for each year of each animal's life span. (For example, measure 65 cm of yarn to represent the life span of an Indian elephant.) Tape the string to the graph in the appropriate row. **Hint:** Allow string longer than the paper to hang off the edge.

2. Repeat Step 1, labeling the vertical axis "1 cm = 1 year the young stays with its mother" and measure 1 cm of string for each year. **Hint:** The house mouse won't have any string and the Indian elephant will have two strings.

3. Repeat Step 1 using the smaller sheet of construction paper and labeling the vertical axis "1 cm = 1 young born at a time" and measure 1 cm of string for each young born.

4. On another sheet of paper or in your science notebook, answer the following questions: What comparisons can be drawn between the number of offspring born at one time and the time spent with an animal's mother? Based on the information from the graphs, why do you think an opossum has so many young at one time?

Explanation: Most animals go through four stages in their life cycles. How each stage is completed is different from animal to animal. Think about the differences between the animals listed. What other comparisons can you make using the information on these graphs?

Fig. 1

	average life span	average time young stays with mother	average number of young born at one time
Indian elephant	65 years	male 14 years female 50 years	1
camel	50 years	4 years	1
human	75 years	18 years	1
house mouse	2½ months	3 weeks	5
opossum	2 years	3 months	12

Fig. 2

Indian elephant · camel · human · house mouse · opossum

©The Education Center, Inc. • *Science in a Box* • TEC1749

Note to the teacher: Use as directed on page 3.

STUDENT ACTIVITY

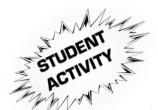

ANIMAL LIFE CYCLES

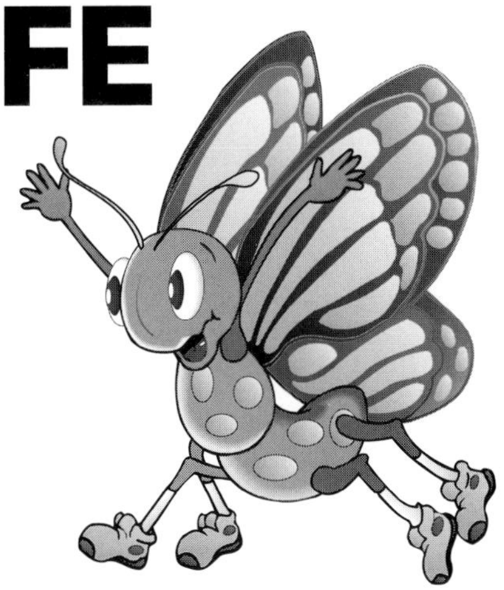

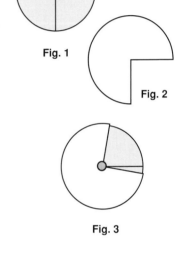

Purpose: to learn about animal life cycles

Animals				
butterfly	frog	stag beetle	human	moth
ladybug beetle	newt	toad		

Procedure:

1. Research to find the life cycles of two of the animals listed in the box above.
2. Use a compass to draw four eight-inch circles on two sheets of 12" x 18" construction paper. Cut out the circles.
3. On two of the circles, draw lines to divide the circle into fourths (Fig. 1). On one of these circles, draw and color the stages of the life cycle of the first animal you chose. Label each stage. Repeat with the second animal you chose.
4. Cut out one-fourth of the other two circles (Fig. 2). Write the names and draw illustrations of the animals you chose on one side of each circle. Place each one of these circles, picture side up, on top of each of the life cycle circles. Carefully insert a metal brad through the center of each set of circles to assemble your life cycle wheels (Fig. 3).

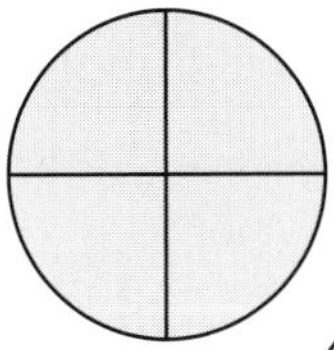

Fig. 1

Fig. 2

Fig. 3

Questions:

1. Compare and contrast each stage of the two life cycles you chose.

   Stage 1 ______________________________

   ____

   Stage 2 ______________________________

   ____

   Stage 3 ______________________________

   ____

   Stage 4 ______________________________

   ____

2. What stage of the human life cycle are you in right now? ______________________________

   Compare this to the same stage of one of the animals you chose. ______________________________

   ____

Explanation: Most organisms go through stages of life. These stages make up an organism's life cycle. Some organisms go through *complete metamorphosis,* or a great body change. Other organisms look very much like their parents and will change in size as they mature.

Note to the teacher: Use as directed on page 3.

BEHAVIOR

Students will be on their best behavior while engaged in this
Science in a Box *unit on behavior!*

Objective: to learn how internal and external stimuli can affect an organism's behavior

Materials: mitten, 2 thermometers, 3 rulers, clear packaging tape

Teacher preparation:
1. Follow the directions on page 3 to assemble your *Science in a Box* unit.
2. Place the items from the materials list above inside the shoebox.

Background Information

The ways in which living things respond to their environment is called *behavior*. Behavior can depend on internal cues, such as hunger, or external cues, such as weather changes. When an animal feels hunger, it will react by searching or hunting for food. If the temperature increases, an animal may find shade to remain cool. If the temperature decreases, an animal may shiver, an action which helps the body warm up.

Answer Key for Student Activity

1. the mittened hand
2. Responses will vary. One possible response: The mitten helps keep out cold weather and hold in the body's warmth.
3. Responses will vary. One possible response: Some animals will hibernate in a cave or other cozy area for the winter.

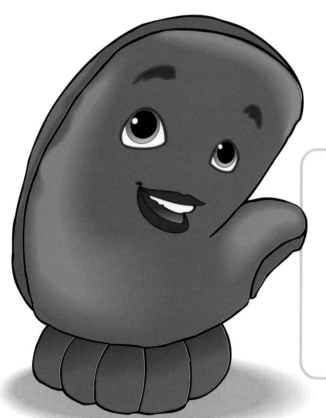

Fabulous Facts

Caribou adapt to the change in temperature by migrating hundreds of miles to find an appropriate winter or summer range.

Black bears in the northern regions can hibernate up to seven months of the year as a way to adapt to the cold and lack of food.

To keep warm, squirrels sometimes wrap their tails around themselves.

LIFE

Behavior

©The Education Center, Inc.

MATERIALS

mitten

2 thermometers

3 rulers

clear packaging tape

SAFETY RULES

1. Do not hold the thermometers too tightly.

2. Use all materials appropriately.

BEHAVIOR CHALLENGER

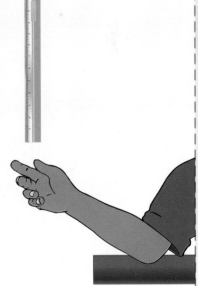

Objective: to learn the effect of external stimuli on behavior

Materials: 3 rulers, clear packaging tape

Procedure:

1. Tape the three rulers together end to end. Ask your partner to put his or her elbow on the edge of a desk as shown. Challenge your partner to catch the rulers as soon as you release them in Step 2.

2. Hold the rulers above your head. Without warning, release the rulers so that they drop straight down. On a separate sheet of paper or in your science notebook, record the ruler (first, second, or third) and the inch mark where your partner's fingers and thumb take hold. Also record if your partner misses. Repeat three times.

3. Predict whether your partner's performance will improve if you give a verbal warning.

4. Repeat Step 2, but as you release the rulers, say, "On your mark. Get set. Drop!" Repeat three times. Record the results.

Explanation: An external stimulation, such as a verbal warning, gives a person or animal time to respond. The response or behavior depends on the stimuli. A person should be able to catch the rulers more quickly when he or she is given a warning. Explain one type of warning an animal might get in the wild and what type of response the animal might have to that warning.

©The Education Center, Inc. • *Science in a Box* • TEC1749

BEHAVIOR

Purpose: to learn how external stimuli can affect an organism's behavior

Procedure:

1. Look at the two pictures below. Predict whether there will be a greater rise in temperature in Figure A or in Figure B.

2. Record your thermometers' temperatures on the chart. Put a mitten on one hand. Gently hold a thermometer in each hand, making sure you are touching the base of the thermometer as shown.

3. On the chart, record each thermometer's temperature every 30 seconds for five minutes.

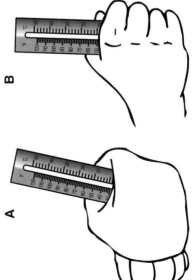

A

B

Time	Hand With Mitten	Hand Without Mitten
Original temperature		
30 seconds		
1 minute		
1 minute 30 seconds		
2 minutes		
2 minutes 30 seconds		
3 minutes		
3 minutes 30 seconds		
4 minutes		
4 minutes 30 seconds		
5 minutes		

Questions:

1. In which hand did the temperature rise less? _____

2. How does a mitten compare to an animal's den or home? _____

3. Based on what you observed with this experiment, how do you think some animals' behaviors change in winter? _____

Explanation: The mitten helped keep your body heat from escaping. In winter, animals find shelter to shield them from the cold. Being in an enclosed area, such as a den or hole in a tree, helps keep an animal warm through the cold winter months. If an animal were in an open area, there wouldn't be anything to block the wind and cold.

Note to the teacher: Use as directed on page 3.

INHERITED CHARACTERISTICS

Your students will inherit a love of science as they complete this Science in a Box *unit on inherited characteristics.*

Objective: to learn about inherited characteristics

Materials: magnifying glass, mirror, class set of 8½" x 11" tagboard or poster board, class set of transparency sheets, permanent fine-tip marker, stapler, crayons or markers

Teacher preparation:
1. Follow the directions on page 3 to assemble your *Science in a Box* unit.
2. Place the items from the materials list above inside the shoebox.
3. Be aware that modifications may need to be made for students who only know one parent or have been adopted.

Background Information

Certain traits are *inherited,* or passed down from our parents in our genes, and some are *environmental,* or affected by the things around us. Inherited traits consist of features such as height, eye color, freckles, dimples, and the ability to roll one's tongue. People can also be influenced by environmental factors based on where and how they live. Environmental factors—such as diet, exercise, and disease—can influence the way genes work.

Fabulous Facts

Gregor Mendel studied heredity about 130 years ago. Some of his methods for studying heredity are still used today.

A person has 46 chromosomes. Twenty-three chromosomes come from the mother and 23 come from the father. Each chromosome contains genes, which determine a person's traits.

Each person has about 50,000 genes! These genes determine height, eye color, and much more.

LIFE
Inherited
Characteristics

MATERIALS

class set of 8½" x 11" tagboard or poster board

class set of transparency sheets

permanent fine-tip marker

stapler   magnifying glass

mirror   crayons or markers

SAFETY RULES

1. Handle the mirror with care.

2. Use all materials appropriately.

INHERITED CHARACTERISTICS CHALLENGER

Objective: to identify inherited characteristics

Materials: magnifying glass, mirror, sheet of tagboard, transparency sheet, permanent marker, stapler, crayons or markers

Procedure:

1. Use the magnifying glass and mirror to look at your physical characteristics. What characteristics do you think you inherited from your parents or grandparents?

2. Draw and color a picture of yourself on the sheet of tagboard.

3. Staple the transparency sheet to your tagboard along the top as shown. Using the permanent marker, label the characteristics you think are inherited.

Explanation: Many of your physical traits are inherited from your parents and grandparents. Skin color, height, nose shape, eye color, freckles, dimples, and hair type and color are all examples of inherited characteristics. On another sheet of paper or in your science notebook, explain how these traits make you who you are.

STUDENT ACTIVITY

INHERITED CHARACTERISTICS

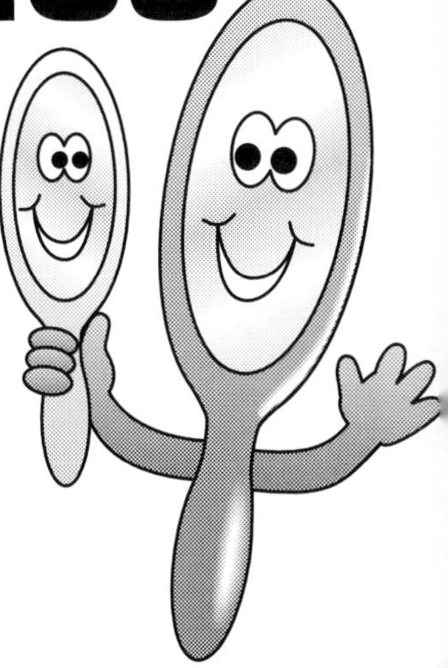

We inherit traits (characteristics) from our parents. Eye and hair color, the shape of our noses and mouths, and hair type are a few examples of inherited characteristics.

Purpose: to learn about inherited characteristics

Procedure:

1. Draw and color a picture of your mother's and father's faces in the first two boxes below.
2. Look in the mirror. Draw and color a picture of your face in the third box.
3. Label the traits in each picture, such as eye color, eye size, nose shape, hair color (dark or blond), type of hair (curly or straight), lip size, and dimples.
4. Answer the questions that follow.

Mom	**Dad**	**Me**

Questions:

1. Which traits do you have in common with your mom? ______________________________
____
2. Which traits do you have in common with your dad? ______________________________
____
3. Which traits do you have in common with both parents? ______________________________
____

Explanation: Every person has 46 chromosomes. Twenty-three come from the mother and 23 come from the father. The characteristics you have inherited come from both of your parents. The dominant traits from each parent are the ones you will likely have.

Note to the teacher: Use as directed on page 3.

EXTINCTION

Don't wait too long before trying this Science in a Box
unit on extinction!

Objective: to discover what happens to animal species when they are unable to adapt to changes in their habitats

Materials: reference books, class supply of U.S. outline maps, colored pencils, 10 index cards

Teacher preparation:
1. Follow the directions on page 3 to assemble your *Science in a Box* unit.
2. Make five habitat cards with a different place listed on each: Arctic tundra, temperate forests, ponds, coral reefs, and grasslands.
3. Make five wildlife cards with animals listed on one side and habitat changes on the other: caribou, temperature increases; squirrels, forests cut down; great crested newts, environment becomes dryer; clownfish, coral reef destroyed; barn owls, temperature drops. (If desired, laminate the cards.)
4. Place the cards and the items from the materials list above inside the shoebox.

Background Information

Extinction is when a *species,* or all of one kind of plant or animal, dies out. When a habitat changes, the affected species must adapt to the change or the chance of extinction increases. A single loss of species can have an effect on a habitat because many plants and animals are dependent on each other. A habitat also has a limit on the number of animals it can support. Limiting factors include the amount of food and water available, pollution, and the number of predators.

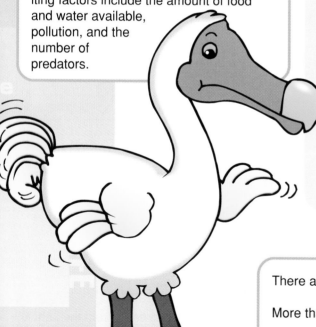

Answer Key for Student Activity

Data Sheet:
Responses for the "Characteristics" and "Adaptation Needed" sections will vary. Possible responses:

Species	Habitat	Characteristics	Change	Adaptation Needed
caribou	Arctic tundra	thick fur, broad hooves	temperature increases	grow less fur
squirrels	temperate forests	live in and around trees	forests cut down	adjust to life around people
great crested newts	ponds	amphibious	environment becomes dryer	live more on land
clownfish	coral reefs	eat algae that grow on the coral reef	coral reefs destroyed	find other source of food or move
barn owls	grasslands	no fat stored for mild winters	temperature drops	store fat for cold winters

Questions:
Responses will vary. Possible responses:
1. Animals are successful in their habitats because they have adapted to that environment.
2. If the habitat changes, a species must adjust to the change.
3. If a species can't or doesn't adjust to changes in its habitat, it could become extinct.
4. Today the main cause of habitat changes is human influence on the environment.

Fabulous Facts

There are more than 1,000 endangered animal species in the world today.

More than 38 million acres of tropical rain forest are destroyed each year.

It is thought that over 500 species, subspecies, and varieties of plants and animals in the United States have become extinct since the Pilgrims landed at Plymouth Rock.

LIFE

Extinction

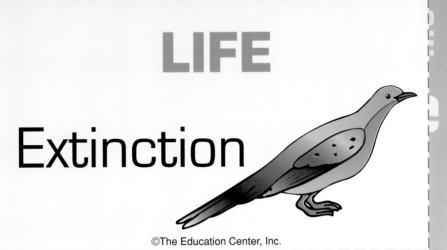

©The Education Center, Inc.

MATERIALS

reference books

class supply of U.S. outline maps

colored pencils

wildlife cards

habitat cards

SAFETY RULE

Use all materials appropriately.

EXTINCTION CHALLENGER

Objective: to show how an animal's range changes as its numbers decrease

Materials: reference books, U.S. outline map, colored pencils

Procedure:

1. Research the American bison, also called the buffalo, or the Florida panther.

2. On the U.S. map, shade in the animal's *current range,* or where the animal lives.

3. Using a different color, shade in the animal's *historic range,* or where the animal used to live.

4. On another sheet of paper or in your science notebook, answer the following questions: How has the range of the animal changed? What do you think caused this animal to lose its population and range? What can people do to build, or continue to build, the animal's numbers?

Explanation: There are many factors that lead to an animal becoming endangered or extinct. One of the most devastating factors is human influence. Humans are responsible for loss of habitats, wildlife trade, overhunting, and bringing domestic and nonnative animals to an area.

©The Education Center, Inc. • *Science in a Box* • TEC1749

Name _____ *Life science: extinction*

EXTINCTION

Purpose: to imagine what animals might do to survive as their habitats change

Procedure:
1. Match each species on the wildlife cards to its corresponding habitat card. Record them on the data sheet.
2. On the data sheet, list the characteristics of each animal that help it live and grow in that habitat. If necessary, use reference materials.
3. Choose one animal from a wildlife card. Flip the card over to see how its habitat could change. Record it on the data sheet.
4. Think about how the animal would have to adapt in order to survive in its changed habitat. Write your ideas on the data sheet.
5. Repeat Steps 3–4 with each wildlife card.

Data Sheet

Species	Habitat	Characteristics	Change	Adaptation Needed
1.				
2.				
3.				
4.				
5.				

Questions:

1. What makes animals successful at living in their habitats? _____

_____

2. What can happen to a species if its habitat changes? _____

_____

3. What happens if a species can't adapt to its new habitat? _____

_____

4. What do you think is the main cause of habitat changes today and is, therefore, most threatening to animals?

_____

_____

Explanation: Species must be able to adapt to changes in their habitats. If they cannot adapt, then they could become extinct. There are many kinds of adaptations. Deer have adapted to people moving into their habitats by eating grass from backyards or corn from cornfields. Arctic hares adjust to seasonal changes by growing white fur in winter to hide them in the snow.

VERTEBRATES AND INVERTEBRATES

Put a little backbone into your science lesson with this
Science in a Box *unit on vertebrates and invertebrates!*

Objective: to learn about vertebrates and invertebrates through hands-on activities

Materials: worm, snail, frog, lizard, 4 transparent containers with lids

Teacher preparation:
1. Follow the directions on page 3 to assemble your *Science in a Box* unit.
2. Poke airholes in the container lids using a sharpened pencil, nail, etc.
3. Place the containers inside the shoebox.
4. On the day of the activities, place one of the animals in each container and secure all the lids.

Background Information

Vertebrates are animals with backbones. *Invertebrates* are animals without backbones. There are about 40,000 species of vertebrates. They are divided into eight classes. Invertebrates are divided into groups called *phyla*. Invertebrates have tough skin, strong shells, or hard, armorlike coverings called *exoskeletons* to support their bodies.

Answer Key for Student Activity

Observations:
Responses will vary. Accept all reasonable responses.
Questions:
Responses will vary. Possible responses:
1. The animals are different in how they move, feel, and look. They are similar in that the vertebrates both have backbones and the invertebrates do not.
2. The frog and lizard can walk and jump like some other vertebrates, and they have backbones.
3. The worm and snail are moist like some other invertebrates, and they do not have backbones.

Fabulous Facts

More than 90 percent of the world's animals are invertebrates!

There are more than 1 million different kinds of invertebrates!

Fish are vertebrates. There are over 30,000 different kinds of fish!

LIFE

Vertebrates and Invertebrates

MATERIALS

worm   frog

snail   lizard

4 transparent containers with lids

SAFETY RULES

1. Handle all animals carefully and appropriately.

2. Wash your hands before and after touching the animals.

VERTEBRATES AND INVERTEBRATES CHALLENGER

Objective: to compare the human backbone with the backbone of other vertebrates and the physical support systems of invertebrates

Materials: worm, snail, frog, lizard, 4 transparent containers with lids

Procedure:

1. Observe the backbones of the frog and lizard. Notice that the worm and snail do not have backbones. What does the snail have instead?

2. Feel your backbone with your hand. On another sheet of paper or in your science notebook, explain how your backbone compares to those of other vertebrates.

Explanation: All vertebrates have a backbone. When you run your fingers down your spine, you can feel the *vertebrae,* or bones of the backbone. Invertebrates do not have backbones. Instead, they have tough skin, strong shells, or hard, armorlike coverings to support their bodies.

VERTEBRATES AND INVERTEBRATES

Do you have a backbone? Of course you do—you are a vertebrate! Animals without backbones are invertebrates.

Purpose: to learn about vertebrates and invertebrates

Procedure:

1. Observe how the vertebrates (frog and lizard) and invertebrates (worm and snail) move. Record your observations on the chart below.
2. Feel the back of each animal. Record what you feel on the chart.
3. Touch the skin of each animal. Record how the skin feels on the chart.

Observations

Animal	Movement	Back	Skin
frog			
lizard			
worm			
snail			

Questions:

1. In what ways are these animals different? _____

    _____

    How are they similar? _____

    _____

2. How are the two vertebrates like other vertebrates, such as fish and mammals (including humans)?

    _____

    _____

3. How are the invertebrates like other invertebrates, such as jellyfish, clams, and spiders?

    _____

    _____

Explanation: Vertebrates have backbones. Invertebrates do not have backbones. Instead of a backbone, invertebrates have tough skin, strong shells, or hard, armorlike coverings called exoskeletons to support their bodies.

©The Education Center, Inc. • *Science in a Box* • TEC1749 • Key p. 88

CIRCULATORY SYSTEM

Circulate among your students as they complete this fun
Science in a Box *unit on the circulatory system.*

Objective: to learn about the circulatory system

Materials: stopwatch, class supply of 20 oz. clear plastic cups, measuring cups, spoon, yellow food coloring, $7/8$ c. tomato paste per student, $1/8$ c. milk per student, water

Teacher preparation:
1. Follow the directions on page 3 to assemble your *Science in a Box* unit.
2. Place the items from the materials list above inside the shoebox, except the tomato paste, milk, and water.
3. On the day of the student activity, have the tomato paste, milk, and water available for students.

Background Information

The circulatory system consists of the heart, blood, and blood vessels. The *arteries* are the largest blood vessels. They transport blood from the heart to the rest of the body. *Veins* transport blood back to the heart. The *capillaries* are the smallest blood vessels. They link the arteries and the veins. The blood has many jobs. It moves food and oxygen to the cells and carries wastes away. The blood also keeps the body warm, fights germs, and seals wounds in the skin.

Fabulous Facts

There are hundreds of times more red blood cells in the human body than there are stars in the Milky Way galaxy!

The heart beats about 70 times per minute and about 37 million times per year!

There are about 62,000 miles of blood vessels in an adult's body!

Capillaries are so narrow that only one red blood cell can flow through at a time!

Answer Key for Student Activity

1. yellow water—plasma, tomato paste—red blood cells, milk—white blood cells and platelets
2. The mixture is red. Responses to the other questions will vary.
3. Responses will vary. One possible response: The red blood cells give blood its red color.

LIFE
Circulatory System

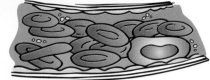

©The Education Center, Inc.

MATERIALS

stopwatch

class supply of 20 oz. clear plastic cups

measuring cups

spoon

yellow food coloring

7/8 c. tomato paste per student

1/8 c. milk per student

water

SAFETY RULES

1. Do not eat or drink the tomato paste, milk, or water used in this experiment.

2. Use all materials appropriately.

CIRCULATORY SYSTEM CHALLENGER

Objective: to learn about how the heart beats at different rates
Materials: stopwatch
Procedure:

1. On another sheet of paper or in your science notebook, copy the Heart Log as shown.

2. Take your pulse rate by placing two fingers on your wrist and then moving them around until you feel your pulse, or heartbeat. Count the number of beats you feel in 15 seconds. Use the stopwatch to time yourself or have a partner keep track of the time for you. Write the number of beats on the chart.

3. Multiply the number of beats by four to get your pulse rate for one minute. Record this on the chart.

4. Complete the chart by doing the activities for the amount of time listed and then calculating your pulse rate per minute.

Heart Log

Activity	Heartbeats in 15 seconds	Multiply by 4	Pulse Rate per Minute
initial pulse rate		x 4	
jumping jacks (2 minutes)		x 4	
rest (5 minutes)			
reading a book (5 minutes)		x 4	
sitting down and standing up (3 minutes)		x 4	

Explanation: Your heart beats at different rates, depending on your actions. You can feel your *pulse,* or heartbeat, any place on your body where an artery is located over cartilage or bone. One of the easiest places to take your pulse is inside your wrist. When was your pulse the fastest? When was it the slowest? Explain why you think your pulse changed the way it did.

©The Education Center, Inc. • *Science in a Box* • TEC1749

CIRCULATORY SYSTEM

Purpose: to learn about the blood

Plasma is the fluid part of blood. It is 90 percent water. *Red blood cells* carry oxygen to all parts of your body. *White blood cells* fight disease. *Platelets* help in blood clotting. Blood is made up of about 54 percent plasma, 45 percent red blood cells, and 1 percent white blood cells and platelets. So why is it red? Conduct the following experiment to find out!

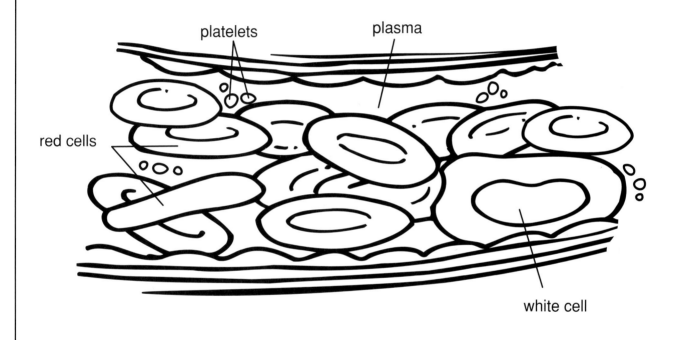

platelets   plasma

red cells

white cell

Procedure:
1. Pour one cup of water into a clear plastic cup. Add two drops of yellow food coloring.
2. Add seven-eighths cup of tomato paste to the cup.
3. Add one-eighth cup of milk to the cup.
4. Stir the mixture to combine the ingredients.

Questions:
1. What does each ingredient represent? (*Hint:* Compare the percentages in the paragraph above with the amount of each ingredient added to the mixture.) _____

_____

2. What color is the mixture? _____ Does this surprise you? _____ Why or why not?

_____

3. Based on the results of the experiment, why do you think blood is red? _____

_____

©The Education Center, Inc. • *Science in a Box* • TEC1749 • Key p. 92

DIGESTIVE SYSTEM

Students will be absorbed in this Science in a Box *unit on the digestive system!*

Objective: to learn about the human digestive system and how it works

Materials: baby food jar with lid; 4 mints or uncoated hard candies for each student; class supply of coffee filters; 2 plastic cups; funnel; measuring spoons; spices, such as basil and oregano; sugar; water; vinegar

Teacher preparation:
1. Follow the directions on page 3 to assemble your *Science in a Box* unit.
2. Place the items from the materials list above inside the shoebox, except the water and vinegar.
3. On the day of each activity, have water available for students.
4. On the day of the student activity, have vinegar available for students.

Background Information

Food is full of the nutrients that our bodies need to live. How does an apple become nourishment for our bodies? It has to be broken down into small particles of nutrients for the body to absorb. Teeth first break the food into smaller pieces. The food then moves down the esophagus to the stomach. In the stomach the food is churned and mixed with digestive juices that continue to break it down. The food passes from the stomach into the small intestine. After chemicals from the pancreas and kidney break down the food even further, the small intestine absorbs the needed nutrients and passes the rest to the large intestine, which gets rid of the waste.

Answer Key for Student Activity

1. The pieces of mint in the vinegar were the quickest to dissolve. Responses to the second part of the question will vary.
2. water–saliva, vinegar–digestive juices, shaking–movement of the stomach

Fabulous Facts

Gastric juices in the stomach can dissolve just about any tissue, but the mucus in the stomach protects the organ from any harm.

An average-sized male eats over 30 tons of food in his lifetime.

The small intestine can be about 22 feet long, and the large intestine can be about five feet long.

Food can remain in the stomach for two to five hours.

LIFE

Digestive System

MATERIALS

baby food jar with lid
4 mints or uncoated hard candies for each student
class supply of coffee filters
2 plastic cups
funnel
measuring spoons
spices
sugar
water
vinegar

SAFETY RULES

1. Do not eat the candy or spices or drink the liquid used in the activities.

2. Handle the glass jars with care.

3. Use all materials appropriately.

DIGESTIVE SYSTEM CHALLENGER

Objective: to learn about how the small intestine works

Materials: coffee filter, 2 plastic cups, funnel, spices, measuring spoons, sugar, water

Procedure:

1. Fill one of the cups halfway with water. Add one tablespoon of sugar and one teaspoon of spices. Stir until the sugar dissolves.

2. Place a coffee filter inside the funnel and place the funnel in the other cup as shown.

3. Pour the water mixture through the filter and into the cup. What is left in the filter? What has gone through the filter?

Explanation: The final stages of digestion take place in the small intestine where food is broken down further by digestive juices. Fully digested food is *absorbed,* or taken in, by the small intestine and passed into the bloodstream to be used by the body. Waste will pass on to the large intestine. On another sheet of paper or in your science notebook, explain what the filter, sugar water, and spices represent in the process of digestion.

Note to the teacher: Use as directed on page 3.

DIGESTIVE SYSTEM

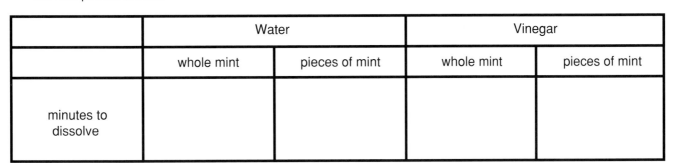

Purpose: to learn about the human digestive system and how it works

Procedure:

1. Do you think a mint will dissolve faster in water or vinegar?

   _____

   Do you think a mint will dissolve faster if it is whole or in pieces?

   _____

2. Fill the jar halfway with water.
3. Add a mint to the jar and put the lid on securely. Keep track of the time as you shake the jar until the mint is dissolved. Record on the chart the amount of time it takes to dissolve the mint. Empty the jar.
4. Break a mint into several small pieces. Repeat Steps 2 and 3 with the pieces of mint.
5. Fill the jar halfway with vinegar. Repeat Step 3.
6. Break a mint into several small pieces. Fill the jar halfway with vinegar. Repeat Step 3 with the pieces of mint.

	Water		Vinegar	
	whole mint	pieces of mint	whole mint	pieces of mint
minutes to dissolve				

Questions:

1. In which test did the mint dissolve the fastest? _____

   Was your prediction correct? _____

2. Which part of the digestive system is represented by the water? _____

   By the vinegar? _____ By shaking the jar? _____

Explanation: The body must break down food into units small enough to be used. The process begins with the teeth and the tongue breaking the food into smaller pieces. Saliva and digestive juices then break down the food in the stomach as the muscles churn or mix the food and digestive juices.

Take a deep breath and let the science flow with this
Science in a Box *unit on the respiratory system.*

Objective: to understand how the diaphragm and the lungs work together when we breathe

Materials: class supply of clean, empty 20 oz. plastic bottles; 2 drinking straws per student; two 12" balloons per student; two 7" balloons per student; masking tape; modeling clay; scissors; tape measure

Teacher preparation:
1. Follow the directions on page 3 to assemble your *Science in a Box* unit.
2. Ahead of time, cut off the bottom two-thirds of the plastic bottles. Cover the edges with masking tape.
3. Place the items from the materials list above inside the shoebox, except the plastic bottles.
4. On the day of the student activity, place the bottles with the shoebox.

Background Information

Breathing involves two main actions: *inhaling,* which pulls air into the lungs, and *exhaling,* which pushes air out of the lungs. The lungs' movement results mainly from the contractions of a large muscle forming the floor of the chest cavity: the *diaphragm.* As the diaphragm contracts, the chest expands and air rushes in through the nose and mouth; as it relaxes, the chest shrinks, pushing air out.

Answer Key for Student Activity

Responses will vary. Possible responses:
1. The smaller balloons act like the lungs. The larger balloon acts like the diaphragm. When the larger balloon is pulled down, the smaller balloons are inflated. When the larger balloon is pushed up, the smaller balloons deflate.
2. Air enters the lungs when the diaphragm moves down. Air leaves the lungs when the diaphragm moves up.
3. The balloons wouldn't be able to fill with as much air. Smoking or inhaling other pollutants might cause this in real life.

Fabulous Facts

Each day the average person inhales and exhales about 24,000 times. If he lives to be 70, he will have taken about 600 million breaths!

A ten-year-old takes about 20 breaths per minute while an adult takes between 6 and 12 breaths per minute.

Oxygen is vital for life, but it is possible to have too much. Pure oxygen is about five times stronger than the amount of oxygen found in air.

LIFE

Respiratory System

©The Education Center, Inc.

MATERIALS

class supply of clean, empty 20 oz. plastic bottles
2 drinking straws per student
two 12" balloons per student
two 7" balloons per student
masking tape
modeling clay
scissors
tape measure

SAFETY RULES

1. Stop blowing air into the balloon if you begin to feel lightheaded.

2. Discard the balloon in the challenger activity after it has been used.

3. Use all materials appropriately.

RESPIRATORY SYSTEM CHALLENGER

Objective: to observe lung capacity
Materials: 12" balloon, tape measure
Procedure:
1. Stretch the balloon several times.
2. Exhale normally. Then blow the air that is left in your lungs into the balloon.
3. Pinch the end of the balloon and have a partner help you measure the *circumference,* or distance around the balloon. Record the measurement on another sheet of paper or in your science notebook.
4. Perform the experiment two more times. Why do you think you were able to blow up the balloon after you exhaled?

Explanation: Some air remains in our lungs even after we exhale. That air is called *reserve air volume.* A person's reserve air volume is the amount of air left in the lungs after a normal exhalation.

RESPIRATORY SYSTEM

Purpose: to understand how the lungs and diaphragm work together

Procedure:

1. Cut off the mouth of the larger balloon. Then fit it over the bottom of the bottle. If necessary, secure the balloon with tape.

2. Tape both smaller balloons to the straws (Fig. 1).

3. Place the balloon ends of the straws in the bottle. Position the straws so that a few inches of each straw sticks out of the bottle (Fig. 2).

4. Secure the straws by positioning the clay around and into the opening of the bottle (Fig. 3).

5. Predict what will happen to the small balloons if you pull down and then push up on the larger balloon.

_____

_____

6. Pull down and then push up on the larger balloon. What happens to the smaller balloons?

_____

_____

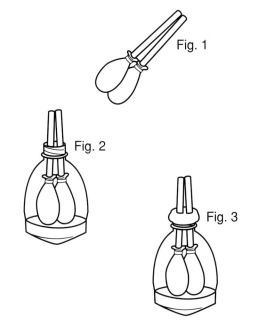

Fig. 1

Fig. 2

Fig. 3

Questions:

1. How does this model work? _____

_____

2. Based on how the model works, how do you think the lungs and diaphragm work together when you breathe? _____

_____

_____

3. What would happen if the smaller balloons were dirty or partially filled with loose particles? _____

_____

What might cause this in real life? _____

_____

Explanation: Because lungs aren't muscles, they can't move by themselves. Instead, they work with a large muscle at the bottom of the chest cavity called the *diaphragm.* When inhalation occurs, the diaphragm changes the volume of the chest cavity, causing the lungs to expand.

NERVOUS SYSTEM

Don't be nervous! Your students will get the message with this
Science in a Box *unit on the nervous system!*

Objective: to explore the human nervous system and how it works

Materials: blindfold, 2 sets of 5 lunch-size paper bags, 4 index cards, 2 scented markers (different scents), ice pack, small rock, class supply of paper towel tubes, class supply of 12" x 18" sheets of construction paper, class supply of flavored candy (half of one flavor and half of another flavor), scissors, tape, yarn

Teacher preparation:
1. Follow the directions on page 3 to assemble your *Science in a Box* unit.
2. Number the bags in each set from 1 to 5. Prepare the bags as follows:
   Bag 1: Put a scented marker in each bag.
   Bag 2: Put one type of flavored candy in each bag.
   Bag 3: Put a rock in one bag and an ice pack in the other.
   Bag 4: On an index card write instructions for a student to make clapping and snapping noises. On a second card, write instructions for a student to make paper rustling and feet shuffling noises. Place one card in each bag.
   Bag 5: Copy each optical illusion and question to the right on a separate index card. Write the answers on the backs of the cards. Place one card in each bag.
3. Seal the bags with tape. Then place the bags and the items from the materials list above inside the shoebox, except the paper towel tubes.
4. On the day of the student activity, place the paper towel tubes with the shoebox materials.
5. On the day of the challenger activity, pair students to complete the activity.

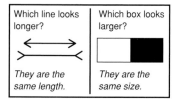

Which line looks longer?	Which box looks larger?
They are the same length.	They are the same size.

Background Information

The nervous system tells what is happening inside and outside the body. Its command center is the brain. Branching nerves run throughout the body carrying messages to the brain and receiving messages from the sense organs. The nerves in the body act like telephone wires. Once impulses reach the brain, the brain decides how to respond and then sends impulses on how to react.

Answer Key for Student Activity

1. The yarn represents the nerves.
2. The path should be traced back because once the brain receives the message that something hot is being touched, it sends a message back to the hand to tell it to pull away.

Fabulous Facts

The brain has 12 billion cells constantly receiving and sending messages by way of the nerves.

Nerves are different sizes. Some nerves reach from your toes all the way up to your brain.

The spinal cord, inside the backbone, is the major highway carrying nerve impulses from our senses to our brain. All the nerves join this highway before reaching the brain.

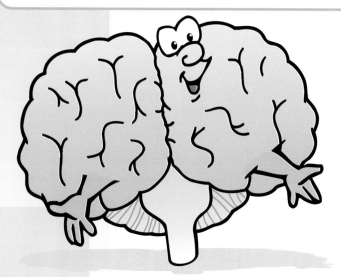

LIFE

Nervous System

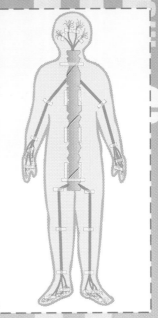

©The Education Center, Inc.

MATERIALS

scissors   yarn

tape

blindfold

2 sets of 5 sealed lunch-size paper bags

class supply of paper towel tubes

class supply of 12" x 18" construction paper

SAFETY RULES

1. In the challenger activity, do not tie the blindfold so tightly that it hurts the person wearing it.

2. Use all materials appropriately.

NERVOUS SYSTEM CHALLENGER

Objective: to learn how the nervous system and the senses work together

Materials: blindfold, 2 sets of 5 sealed lunch-size paper bags

Procedure:

1. Do not look in the bags. Give one set of five bags to your partner and keep the other set.
2. On another sheet of paper or in your science notebook, copy the chart as shown.
3. Blindfold your partner. Record his or her name on the chart.
4. Take the item out of each bag, in turn, as you follow the steps below to conduct the experiment. Record your partner's response to each bag's contents on the chart.

    Bag 1: Have your partner smell the item and try to figure out what scent it is.
    Bag 2: Have your partner taste the item and try to figure out what flavor it is.
    Bag 3: Have your partner feel the item and try to figure out what it is.
    Bag 4: Follow the directions on the card. Have your partner try to figure out what sounds you are making.
    Bag 5: Take the blindfold off your partner. Have your partner try to figure out the optical illusion.

5. Trade places with your partner and repeat Steps 3–4.

Questions: Were you and your partner able to guess all of the items correctly? Which items were easier to figure out? Was one sense more accurate than another?

Explanation: Most of what the brain knows, remembers, and learns comes in through the eyes as words, pictures, and other visual experiences. When you feel something, you feel the contact with skin and other sensations, such as cold or hot and smooth or rough. All of this information is carried by the nerves to your brain.

Data Sheet

	Name _____ Response	Name _____ Response
Bag 1		
Bag 2		
Bag 3		
Bag 4		
Bag 5		

©The Education Center, Inc. • *Science in a Box* • TEC1749

Note to the teacher: Use as directed on page 3.

NERVOUS SYSTEM

Purpose: to learn about the nervous system and how it works

Procedure:

Step 1: Draw and cut out a large person shape from construction paper.

Step 2: Cut a length of yarn long enough to stretch from the head of your shape to the top of the legs. Tape the yarn at the neck and above the legs, leaving about one inch of yarn free at the top. Separate the yarn at the top into four strands and fray the ends. Tape them down as shown.

Step 3: Cut four shorter lengths of yarn. Tape them as shown, fraying the ends for the hands and feet areas.

Step 4: Cut a strip of the paper towel tube long enough to run from the bottom of the shape's head to the top of its legs. Cut an equal number of notches on each side of the strip to represent the spinal column. Lay the tube down the center of your shape, covering the yarn in the middle. Tape it securely.

Step 1: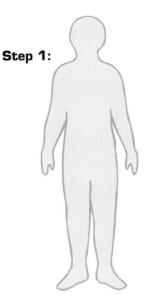

Step 2: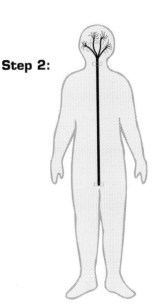

Step 3: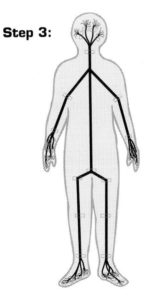

Step 4: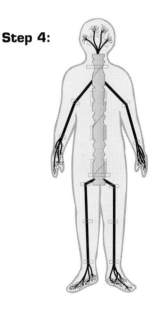

Questions:

1. What does the yarn in the model represent? _____

2. Using the shape, trace the path nerve impulses would follow if you touched something hot. Did you trace the path from the hand to the brain and then back to the hand? _____ Why should you trace the path back to the hand? _____
_____

Explanation: The nervous system is made up of the brain, spinal cord, and nerves. *Neurons,* or nerve cells, receive information from your senses, carry messages from your nervous system to different parts of your body, and send messages between cells. These messages can travel up to 430 feet per second—as fast as a race car!

WATER CYCLE

Dive into science with this Science in a Box
unit on the water cycle!

Objective: to learn about the water cycle through hands-on demonstrations

Materials: cookie sheet; sponge; class supply of construction paper; aluminum foil; small, clear, flat-bottomed bowl; plastic wrap; rubber band; small, resealable plastic bag; watering can; water; 2 ice cubes per student

Teacher preparation:
1. Follow the directions on page 3 to assemble your *Science in a Box* unit.
2. Place the items from the materials list above inside the shoebox, except the cookie sheet, watering can, water, and ice cubes.
3. On the day of the student activity, have the cookie sheet, watering can, and water available for students.
4. On the day of the challenger activity, have water and ice cubes available for students.

Background Information

There is a fixed amount of water on Earth. It moves in a never ending circle called the water, or *hydrologic,* cycle. The cycle is a description of how water continuously moves between the ocean, the sky, and the land.

Like a bicycle wheel, the water cycle doesn't have a beginning or an ending point. Water in the oceans and other bodies of water *evaporates* and enters the atmosphere as water vapor. Then, as the vapor cools, it *condenses,* or changes back into a liquid (water droplets), to form clouds. When the water droplets get larger, gravity pulls the water back to Earth as *precipitation.* Back on the ground, the water begins returning to the ocean. It can do this either through *infiltration,* soaking into the ground, or *runoff,* entering streams along the surface of the land. Both routes end in the ocean—it's a trip that may take many years and include being used by plants, animals, and people. Then the water cycle begins again.

Answer Key for Student Activity

1. The sponge represents better farmland because it soaks up and holds water for plants.
2. a lake
3. a stream or river
4. Responses will vary. Possible responses: The lakes and rivers would eventually dry up and the land would become arid. The land would be unable to support plant growth or provide food for animals.

Fabulous Facts

Scientists estimate that 112 quadrillion gallons of water evaporate from the ocean each year.

About three-fifths of the human body is made up of water!

About 75 percent of precipitation falls into the ocean.

Reno, Nevada, and Phoenix, Arizona, get only eight inches of rain a year. In the same year, Mount Waialeala in Hawaii gets 460 inches of rain!

EARTH
Water Cycle

©The Education Center, Inc.

MATERIALS

cookie sheet

sponge

class supply of construction paper

aluminum foil

small, clear, flat-bottomed bowl

plastic wrap

rubber band

water

small, resealable plastic bag

watering can

2 ice cubes per student

SAFETY RULES

1. Use all materials appropriately.

2. Do not drink any of the water used in the experiments.

WATER CYCLE CHALLENGER

Objective: to demonstrate the water cycle
Materials: clear flat-bottomed bowl, plastic wrap, rubber band, resealable plastic bag, water, 2 ice cubes
Procedure:
1. Pour about a half inch of water into the bottom of the bowl.
2. Cover the bowl with plastic wrap. Secure the wrap with the rubber band.
3. Put two ice cubes into the resealable plastic bag. Seal the bag.
4. Place the bag of ice cubes at the center of the plastic wrap. The wrap should slope into the bowl, but it should not touch the water.
5. Predict what will happen to the ice in the bag and the water in the bowl when you place the bowl in the sun. On another sheet of paper or in your science notebook, record your predictions.
6. Place the bowl in direct sunlight. Observe it every 20 minutes for one hour or until the ice has melted. Record your observations.

Explanation: The sun's heat provides the energy for evaporation to occur. As rising water vapor meets cooler air or a cooler surface, it condenses into liquid form. (This process explains why an ice-cold glass of water will get "sweaty" on a hot summer day. The surface of the glass is much cooler than the air around it. As the warm water vapor hits the glass, the vapor condenses into liquid.) As more and more vapor condenses, some of the water drops eventually grow large enough to fall. What part of the water cycle does the water in the bowl represent? The ice in the bag? The plastic wrap?

©The Education Center, Inc. • *Science in a Box* • TEC1749

WATER CYCLE

Purpose: to show how water infiltration and surface runoff play their parts in the water cycle
Procedure:
1. Set the cookie sheet on a flat surface.
2. Place a sheet of construction paper on the cookie sheet. Fill the bowl with water and place it on the construction paper. Set the damp sponge on the cookie sheet near the bowl. Then use the aluminum foil to form a trough from the bowl to the cookie sheet as shown.
3. With the watering can, sprinkle water evenly around the model. Observe what happens to the water.
4. Draw arrows on the diagram below to show the movement of water from the point it leaves the watering can.

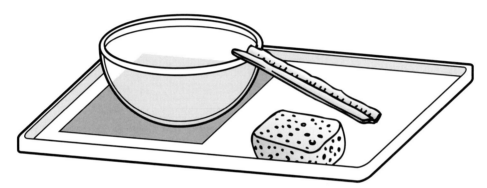

Questions:
1. The construction paper and the sponge represent types of soil. Which one would be better farmland?

   _____ Why? _____

   _____

2. If the cookie sheet represents the ocean, what part of the water cycle does the bowl represent? _____

   _____

3. What part of the water cycle does the aluminum foil represent? _____

   _____

4. If the climate changed and the rainfall stopped, describe what might happen to the "land" represented by the model.

   _____

   _____

   _____

Explanation: Gravity plays a big role in the water cycle process. It pulls water from the sky (precipitation) and causes that water to drain through *infiltration,* or soaking into the ground, and *runoff,* or entering streams along the surface of the land, as it makes its way toward the lowest point, which is usually sea level, or the ocean.

©The Education Center, Inc. • *Science in a Box* • TEC1749 • Key p. 108

ROCKS

Get your science lesson rockin' and rollin' with this
Science in a Box *unit on rocks!*

Objective: to learn about rocks through hands-on activities

Materials: 5 different types of rock samples per student, vinegar, unglazed ceramic tile, eye-dropper, magnifying glass, penny, nail, 2 pieces of white bread per student, class supply of wheat bread, waxed paper, scissors, ruler, heavy book

Teacher preparation:
1. Follow the directions on page 3 to assemble your *Science in a Box* unit.
2. Place the items from the materials list above inside the shoebox, except the bread and the book.
3. On the day of the challenger activity, place the white bread, wheat bread, and book with the shoebox materials.

Background Information

Rocks are the solid parts of the earth. Most rocks are *aggregates,* or combinations, of one or more minerals. There are three main types of rocks: igneous, sedimentary, and metamorphic. *Igneous rocks* are made out of molten volcanic material that cools and hardens. *Sedimentary rocks* are made from dead plant and animal matter. These layers become cemented together over time. *Metamorphic rocks* are formed from igneous and sedimentary rocks that have been put under extreme heat and pressure.

Answer Key for Student Activity

Responses for the rock tests will vary according to the types of rocks used.

Fabulous Facts

The process of erosion can be so slow that it takes a million years for a medium-sized river to move a grain of sand 100 miles downriver.

Rock material that is heated so high that it melts is called magma. It is called lava only when it comes to the surface of the earth, usually through a volcano.

The first tools made by prehistoric people were made from flint, a common stone that splits easily, leaving a sharp edge.

EARTH

Rocks

©The Education Center, Inc.

MATERIALS

5 different types of rock samples

vinegar

unglazed ceramic tile

eyedropper

magnifying glass

penny

nail

2 pieces of white bread per student

class supply of wheat bread

waxed paper

scissors

ruler

heavy book

SAFETY RULES

1. Use all materials appropriately.

2. Do not drink the vinegar used in the student activity.

ROCKS CHALLENGER

Objective: to learn about sedimentary and metamorphic rocks

Materials: 2 pieces of white bread, piece of wheat bread, waxed paper, scissors, ruler, heavy book

Procedure:

1. Lay a sheet of waxed paper on the table or desk. Stack the bread on the waxed paper as shown.

2. Use the ruler to measure the height of the stack. On another sheet of paper or in your science notebook, tell what type of rock the stack represents and why.

3. Lay another sheet of waxed paper on top of the bread. Place the book on top of the stack and press down. Measure the height of the stack. Use the scissors to cut the stack of bread in half. What type of rock does the stack now represent? Explain.

Explanation: Existing rocks can change and become new rocks when heat and pressure are added.

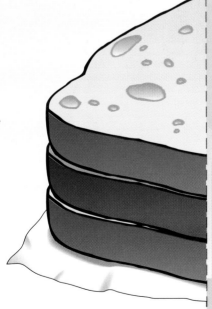

©The Education Center, Inc. • *Science in a Box* • TEC1749

Note to the teacher: Use as directed on page 3.

ROCKS

Purpose: to learn about the different characteristics of rocks

Procedure: Examine each rock using a magnifying glass. Then complete the chart to classify your rocks.

Test	Rock 1	Rock 2	Rock 3	Rock 4	Rock 5
Color (List the colors visible.)					
Streak (Rub the rock on the tile. What is the color of the streak?)					
Texture (Use a magnifying glass to look at the grains or crystals in the rock. Are the grains coarse, fine, or nonexistent?)					
Luster (Does the rock reflect light? Does it have a metallic luster, a glassy luster, or is it dull?)					
Hardness (Scratch the rock with your fingernail, a penny, and then a nail. Which one leaves a mark?)					
Chemical Composition (Use the eyedropper to place a small drop of vinegar on the rock. If the rock bubbles, it contains lime. Tell whether the rock contains lime.)					

Questions:

1. Which rock(s) is the hardest? _____ How do you know? _____

   _____

   _____

2. Which rock(s) has coarse grains? _____

   Which has fine grains? _____

3. Which rock(s) contains lime? _____

4. Are any of your rock samples identical? _____ Explain. _____

   _____

   _____

Explanation: There are three main types of rocks: *igneous, sedimentary,* and *metamorphic.* Rocks are classified by eight characteristics: hardness, color, streak, texture, luster, cleavage (how a rock breaks), chemical composition, and density (the amount of matter in a unit volume of any substance).

LAYERS OF THE EARTH

Peel back the layers of your science lesson with this
Science in a Box *unit on the layers of the earth!*

Objective: to learn about the layers of the earth through hands-on activities

Materials: two 20 cm squares of poster board per student; red, orange, brown, and yellow colored pencils; scissors; tape; hole puncher; string; centimeter ruler; compass; class supply of oranges; plastic knife; reference materials on the layers of the earth

Teacher preparation:
1. Follow the directions on page 3 to assemble your *Science in a Box* unit.
2. Place the items from the materials list above inside the shoebox, except the poster board squares, the oranges, and the reference materials.
3. On the day of the student activity, place the poster board squares and the reference materials with the shoebox materials.
4. On the day of the challenger activity, place the oranges with the other materials.

Background Information

The earth is composed of four layers. The first layer, the *crust,* is the thinnest layer. It is about five miles thick under the oceans and about 25 miles thick under the continents. The second layer, the *mantle,* makes up about four-fifths of the earth's mass. Part of the upper portion of the mantle is semimolten; the lower mantle is solid rock. The mantle is about 1,800 miles thick. The final two layers are divided into the outer and inner cores. The *outer core* is molten material. Scientists believe that it is composed mostly of iron and nickel. The outer core is about 1,300 miles thick. The *inner core* is believed to be a solid mass composed mostly of iron and nickel. The temperature of the inner core may be as high as 11,000°F. Its diameter is about 1,500 miles.

Answer Key for Student Activity

1. mantle, crust
2. The outer core is mostly molten iron and nickel and is about 1,300 miles thick. The inner core is mostly solid iron and nickel and is about 1,500 miles in diameter.
3. The inner core is the hottest with temperatures reaching about 11,000°F.
4. The crust can support life. Responses to the second part of the question may vary. Possible responses: The crust can support life because it is the right temperature, and air, water, and soil are available.

Fabulous Facts

Lava can reach temperatures of 2,200°F!

The earth's crust is broken into large, slowly moving pieces called plates.

The deepest rock samples ever gathered came from 60 miles below the surface!

EARTH

Layers of the Earth

©The Education Center, Inc.

MATERIALS

two 20 cm squares
  of poster board
  per student

red, orange, brown,
  and yellow colored
  pencils

tape

hole puncher

string

scissors

centimeter ruler

compass

class supply of
  oranges

plastic knife

reference materials
  on the layers of
  the earth

SAFETY RULES

1. Use all materials appropriately.

2. Wash your hands before handling the orange.

LAYERS OF THE EARTH CHALLENGER

Objective: to learn about how the crust is made up of plates

Materials: orange, plastic knife

Procedure:

1. Carefully peel the orange, using the plastic knife to get started if necessary. Try to keep the peel of the orange in large pieces. You need at least four pieces.

2. Try to put the peel back together around the orange. Do the pieces fit together perfectly?

3. Push two of the pieces together. On another sheet of paper or in your science notebook explain how the pieces move. Do they push up on each other? Does one slide under the other one? Does one slide past the other?

Explanation: The earth's crust and upper mantle are divided into seven large plates and several smaller plates. These plates move because of currents caused by the differences in temperatures in the earth's interior. These plates move in different directions, causing plates to push against each other, move away from each other, or move past each other. Along these plate boundaries, volcanoes and earthquakes occur. How is the orange peel like the earth's crust?

©The Education Center, Inc. • *Science in a Box* • TEC1749

LAYERS OF THE EARTH

Purpose: to learn about the layers of the earth

Procedure:

1. On a sheet of poster board, use a centimeter ruler and a compass to draw four circles, one inside the next, with the following diameters: 20 cm, 19.8 cm, 10.8 cm, and 3.8 cm. Cut along the 20 cm line. Draw the middle three circles on the back. (Fig. 1)

2. Repeat Step 1 on a second sheet of poster board. Then draw a line from one side of each cutout to the center. Cut along each line. (Fig. 2)

3. Use colored pencils to lightly color each "layer" a different color as follows: outer-most layer—brown, second layer—yellow, third layer—orange, center—red.

4. Research to find the names of the layers of the earth, the thickness of each layer, what each layer consists of, and the temperature of each layer. On the front and back of one cutout, record the name of each layer. On the second cutout, record the name, thickness, composition, and temperature of each layer.

5. Fit the two cutouts together along the cut lines to create a 3-D model of the layers of the earth. Use tape to secure your model if necessary. Punch a hole and tie a length of string to your model so that it can be hung up. (Fig. 3)

6. Use your model to answer the questions.

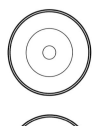

Fig. 1

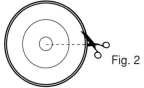

Fig. 2

Fig. 3

Questions:

1. Which layer is the thickest? _____ Thinnest? _____

2. What are the differences between the inner and outer cores? _____

   _____

   _____

   _____

3. Which layer is the hottest? _____ How hot is it? _____

4. Which layer can support life? _____ What factors make this possible? _____

   _____

   _____

Explanation: There are four very distinct layers of the earth. Within the layers there are areas of *molten,* or liquid, rock and areas of solid rock. It is extremely hot inside the earth. The inner core can reach up to 11,000°F!

FOSSILS

Make an impression on students with this Science in a Box *unit on fossils!*

Objective: to learn about fossils and how they're formed

Materials: sugar cubes, glue, Mod Podge sealer, small flat objects (such as pieces of leaves, grass, flower petals, or paper), strainer, bowl, 2-cup measure, paintbrush, 3 chocolate chip cookies per student, class supply of toothpicks and paper towels, eyedropper, water, reference materials on fossils

Teacher preparation:

1. Follow the directions on page 3 to assemble your *Science in a Box* unit.
2. Place the items from the materials list above inside the shoebox, except the reference materials, strainer, bowl, 2-cup measure, cookies, paper towels, and water.
3. The day before the student activity, glue together four sugar cubes to form a square. Then, using a paintbrush, add Mod Podge sealer to one side of the square. Stick a flat object from the list above to the sealer (Fig. 1). Glue another four cubes together and add sealer to one of its sides. Stack the squares so that the object is sealed between them (Fig. 2). Repeat to make a class set. Let the sugar-cube blocks dry overnight.
4. The day of the student activity, place the sugar-cube blocks, strainer, bowl, 2-cup measure, and reference materials with the shoebox supplies. Students will need access to water.
5. On the day of the challenger activity, place the cookies and paper towels with the other supplies.

Fig. 1

Fig. 2

Background Information

A fossil is the recognizable remains of a once living thing that has been preserved, usually in sedimentary rock. In order to become a fossil, an organism or plant needs to be buried quickly so that it can't become completely decomposed or be scavenged by animals. The parts of living organisms that are most likely to become fossils are the hard parts, such as the woody tissue of plants and the shells, bones, and teeth of animals.

Fabulous Facts

Today, the oldest fossils found on Earth are tiny bacteria that some scientists estimate to be 3.5 billion years old!

Chalk, such as the kind your teacher uses, is made up of fossilized shells of a single-celled organism called a foraminifer.

Answer Key for Student Activity

1. Fossils can be found deep within rock layers. Rock can be worn away just as the sugar cubes were.
2. Water in the form of rain or ocean waves can erode rock.
3. Erosion caused by the wind might expose a fossil.
4. Amber is hardened tree resin. The resin remains clear even after it hardens so that anything trapped in it can still be seen in the hardened amber. The glue, like amber, dries clear and helps preserve the object within it.
5. Yes, amber fossils can provide greater learning about past animals and plants because they help preserve them. Most fossils just preserve the bones of an animal, but amber preserves the entire body or structure of the trapped animal or plant.

EARTH

Fossils

©The Education Center, Inc.

MATERIALS

strainer

bowl

2-cup measure

paintbrush

3 chocolate
   chip cookies
   per student

class supply of sugar-
   cube blocks, toothpicks,
   and paper towels

eyedropper

water

reference materials
   on fossils

SAFETY RULES

1. Use all materials appropriately.

2. Do not eat any of the food used in the experiments.

FOSSILS CHALLENGER

Objective: to understand how *paleontologists,* or scientists who study fossil remains, remove fossils from rocks

Materials: paper towel, paintbrush, toothpick, 3 chocolate chip cookies, eyedropper, water

Procedure:

1. Cookie 1: Use a toothpick and a paintbrush to try to remove each chocolate chip without breaking or scratching the chips.
2. Cookie 2: Try to remove each chip using water and a toothpick without breaking or scratching the chips.
3. Cookie 3: Try to remove each chip with your fingers without breaking or scratching the chips.
4. On another sheet of paper or in your science notebook, explain which method worked the best, which worked the worst, and why.

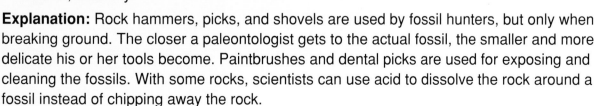

Explanation: Rock hammers, picks, and shovels are used by fossil hunters, but only when breaking ground. The closer a paleontologist gets to the actual fossil, the smaller and more delicate his or her tools become. Paintbrushes and dental picks are used for exposing and cleaning the fossils. With some rocks, scientists can use acid to dissolve the rock around a fossil instead of chipping away the rock.

©The Education Center, Inc. • *Science in a Box* • TEC1749

STUDENT ACTIVITY

FOSSILS

Purpose: to better understand amber fossils

Procedure:

1. There are "fossilized" materials in the centers of the sugar-cube blocks. Look at the pictures below. What do you think will happen when the sugar-cube blocks have water poured over them?

    _____

2. Use the following steps to uncover your "fossil."
    a. Place the strainer over the bowl.
    b. Put the sugar-cube block in the strainer.
    c. Pour water over the sugar-cube block to melt away the sugar. If necessary, empty the water as the bowl becomes full.
    d. Gently use your fingers to rub away some of the excess sugar until you can see your fossil. What is your fossil? _____

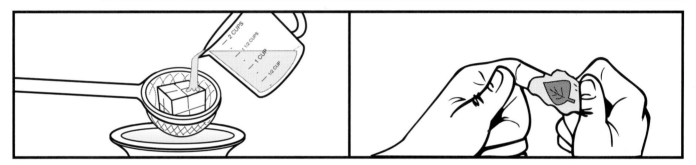

Questions:

1. How is the sugar in the experiment like rock? _____

2. If the sugar is rock, what are two ways in real life that water might erode rock? _____

    _____

3. What other kind of erosion might expose a fossil? _____

4. Research to find out how the glue is like amber. _____

    _____

5. Do amber fossils provide greater learning about the animals and plants of our past than other fossils? _____

    Explain. _____

    _____

    _____

    _____

Explanation: Amber fossils are created when tree resin drips over and traps an insect, a small animal, or a piece of plant. Over time the amber hardens, preserving the entire specimen. Amber fossils provide scientists with almost perfect animals and plants from Earth's history. It allows them to get a glimpse into some of the animals' behavior as well as the kinds of plants that existed at that time.

THE SUN'S ENERGY

Serve your next science lesson sunny-side up with this
Science in a Box *unit on the sun's energy!*

Objective: to learn about the importance of the sun's energy

Materials: waxed paper, cloth, felt, construction paper, scissors, glue, tape, small ball of clay, toothpicks, lamp with at least a 60-watt bulb, stopwatch, 2 pieces of chocolate candy per student, flashlight, class supply of white paper, ruler

Teacher preparation:
1. Follow the directions on page 3 to assemble your *Science in a Box* unit.
2. Place the items from the materials list above inside the shoebox, except the lamp.
3. On the day of the student activity, place the lamp with the other materials.

Background Information

All life on Earth depends on the sun for heat, light, and food. Energy from the sun is responsible for all of the weather on the earth. Sunlight helps plants make food through photosynthesis. The earth's atmosphere helps the earth retain the sun's heat. Because the earth's surface is curved, some areas receive more heat and light than other areas. The sun's rays are more concentrated around the equator and more spread out toward the North and South Poles.

Answer Key for Student Activity

1. The candy outside the shelter melts faster than the candy inside the shelter because the shelter provides some protection from the lamp (sun).
2. Responses will vary. The felt is the best shelter from the heat.
3. Animals need shade or shelter from the sun because their body temperatures can become too high.

Fabulous Facts

The fossil fuels coal, petroleum, and natural gas contain stored solar energy from millions of years ago.

It takes about eight minutes for light from the sun to reach the earth.

Every 40 minutes the sun delivers as much energy to the earth as all the people on the earth use in one year.

The sun is about 4,600,000,000 years old and will probably be a source of energy for another five billion years!

EARTH
The Sun's Energy

©The Education Center, Inc.

MATERIALS

waxed paper
cloth
felt
construction paper
scissors
glue
tape
small ball of clay

toothpicks
lamp
stopwatch
2 pieces of chocolate candy per student
flashlight
class supply of white paper
ruler

SAFETY RULES

1. Use all materials appropriately.
2. Do not look directly at the sun.

THE SUN'S ENERGY CHALLENGER

Objective: to learn why some areas of the earth receive more heat and light than other areas
Materials: flashlight, sheet of white paper, ruler
Procedure:

1. Fold the paper in half; then unfold it. Hold the flashlight about 12 inches directly over one half of the paper. Turn the flashlight on. Trace the outline of the light shining on the paper.
2. Repeat Step 1, but hold the flashlight at a 45° angle about 12 inches above the opposite side of the paper.
3. On another sheet of paper or in your science notebook, explain why the outlines you drew were different. How is the flashlight like the sun? How is the paper like the earth? Use what you have observed to explain what part of the earth would receive the most heat and light from the sun.

Explanation: The sun's rays are more concentrated around the equator and more spread out toward the North and South Poles. Tropical regions near the equator are hotter than the regions near the poles because the sun shines almost directly over the equator at noon. It never rises far above the horizon at the Poles.

©The Education Center, Inc. • *Science in a Box* • TEC1749

THE SUN'S ENERGY

Purpose: to learn about the sun as a heat source

Procedure:

1. Use the materials listed below to construct a shelter that will protect your animal (chocolate candy) from the sun's (lamp's) heat.
   Rules: You may use any of the items listed. You do not have to use all of the items. You must be able to see your candy during the experiment.

waxed paper	felt	scissors	tape
cloth	construction paper	glue	toothpicks
small ball of clay			

2. After constructing your shelter, place it under the lamp. Place one piece of chocolate candy inside your shelter and one outside the shelter. Turn the lamp on, making sure the light shines on the shelter and the candy outside the shelter. Predict how long it will take each piece of candy to begin to melt.

   candy inside the shelter _____

   candy outside the shelter _____

3. To test your predictions, turn the lamp on and use a stopwatch to keep track of the amount of time it takes the chocolate candy to begin to melt. (Touch the candy each minute. When it squishes, stop the timer.) Record your results.

   candy inside the shelter _____

   candy outside the shelter _____

Questions:

1. Which piece of candy melted faster? _____ Why? _____

   _____

   _____

2. Do you think one of the other materials would have made a better shelter from the heat? _____

   If so, which one and why? If not, why? _____

   _____

   _____

3. Why do you think it is necessary for animals to have shelter from the sun? _____

   _____

   _____

Explanation: Heat, light, and other kinds of energy come from the sun. People, animals, and plants depend on this energy. The heat from the sun can also be damaging. Some animals will find shade or shelter if their body temperatures get too hot.

COMETS

Take a trip around the solar system with this
Science in a Box *unit on comets!*

Objective: to learn about comets through hands-on activities

Materials: class supply of brown flat-bottomed coffee filters and rubber bands, plastic wrap, sand, pebbles, roll of white crepe paper, roll of blue crepe paper, ruler, scissors, tape, tablespoon, compass, centimeter ruler, fan, reference materials on comets

Teacher preparation:
1. Follow the directions on page 3 to assemble your *Science in a Box* unit.
2. Place the items from the materials list above inside the shoebox, except the fan and the reference materials.
3. On the day of the student activity, place the fan and reference materials with the other materials. Plug in the fan. Then lay a ruler perpendicular to it, centering the one-inch line under the fan head.

Background Information

Comets have a solid center, or *nucleus,* composed mostly of ice and rocky dust; *comas,* or cloudy atmospheres; and one or two tails. The coma is a dusty cloud that forms around the nucleus as the comet's orbit brings it closer to the heat of the sun. As the comet approaches the sun, solar wind blows some of the coma outward, creating one or two tails, which always point away from the sun. A comet tail with a white hue consists of dust particles. A tail with a blue hue consists of gases.

Fabulous Facts

The Great Comet of 1843 had a tail of about 200 million miles in length. It could have wrapped around Earth's equator close to 8,000 times.

Since a comet looks like a star with long hair, its gas and dust cloud is named after the Latin word *coma,* meaning long-haired.

If all of the comets were weighed together, Earth would weigh more.

Answer Key for Student Activity

Observations:
A. The tails flow straight out away from the fan.
B. The tails flow straight out away from the fan.
C. The tails flow away from the fan with less force.
D. The tails flow straight out away from the fan.
E. The tails flow straight out away from the fan.
F. The tails flow away from the fan with less force.

Questions:
1. As the comet got farther from the fan, the tails flowed away from the fan with less force.
2. The direction the comet was facing did not make a difference. The tails always flowed away from the fan.
3. plastic wrap—nucleus, coffee filter—coma, sand and pebbles—dust and rocks in the coma, white crepe paper—dust tail, blue crepe paper—gas tail
4. The fan's wind is like the sun's <u>solar wind</u>, which always pushes the comet's tails <u>away</u> from the sun.

EARTH

Comets

©The Education Center, Inc.

MATERIALS

class supply of brown
  flat-bottomed coffee
  filters and rubber
  bands
plastic wrap
sand
pebbles
roll of white crepe
  paper
roll of blue crepe
  paper

ruler
scissors
tape
tablespoon
compass
centimeter ruler
fan
reference materials
  on comets

SAFETY RULES

1. Use all materials appropriately.

2. Be careful not to poke yourself or others with the compass.

COMETS CHALLENGER

Objective: to learn how comets decrease in size
Materials: compass, centimeter ruler
Procedure:

1. On another sheet of paper or in your science notebook, measure and draw a circle with a 5 centimeter radius (10 cm diameter). Inside that circle, draw three additional circles. Make each circle with a 1-centimeter-shorter radius than the last one drawn.
2. The 10 cm circle represents a 1-kilometer-wide comet. The remaining circles represent the stages the comet goes through as it melts.
3. If 1 cm (distance between each circle) = 100 m (actual distance) and the comet loses 1 m every 75 years, then how many years does it take the comet to lose 100 m? **Hint:** Multiply 75 by 100. Write this amount in the space between the first two circles.
4. Double the answer to Step 3 to find the number of years it will take the comet to shrink down the next 100 m. Record this number between the second and third circles.
5. To find the number of years between the remaining circles, add the answer from Step 3 to each preceding answer.

Explanation: Comets can range in size from 1 to 10 kilometers. As a comet passes near the sun, about 1 meter of surface area melts away. Some comets have short orbits of a few years, bringing them close to the sun more often than comets having longer orbits lasting thousands of years. About how many more years will it take the comet in the example to melt? What is the life span of the comet in the example?

©The Education Center, Inc. • *Science in a Box* • TEC1749

Note to the teacher: Use as directed on page 3.

COMETS

Purpose: to learn about comets

Procedure:

1. To make a comet, bunch up a golf-ball-size piece of plastic wrap. Place it in the center of a coffee filter. Add a tablespoon each of sand and pebbles. Gather the edges of the filter and secure it with a rubber band as shown to create the nucleus.
2. Cut one eight-inch strip each of white and blue crepe paper. Tape one end of each strip to the filter as shown to create tails. Can you predict what will happen to the comet's tails when the comet is held in front of the fan (sun)? Does distance from the fan affect the movement of the tails? Does the direction the comet is facing affect the movement of the tails? Write your predictions on the data sheet.
3. To test your predictions, turn on the fan, rest your elbow on the table, and position the comet as directed in the chart. Record the results.

Data Sheet:

	Prediction	**Results**
A. Hold at the 4" mark, nucleus facing the fan.		
B. Hold at the 6" mark, nucleus facing the fan.		
C. Hold at the 8" mark, nucleus facing the fan.		
D. Hold at the 4" mark, tails facing the fan.		
E. Hold at the 6" mark, tails facing the fan.		
F. Hold at the 8" mark, tails facing the fan.		

Questions:

1. Did the distance from the fan make a difference in the movement of the tails? _____ Explain. _____
   _____

2. Did the direction the comet was facing make a difference in the movement of the tails? _____
   Explain. _____

3. Research to find what part of a comet each item listed below represents.
   plastic wrap _____   sand and pebbles _____
   coffee filter _____   white crepe paper _____   blue crepe paper _____

4. Fill in the blanks. The fan's wind is like the sun's _____ , which always pushes the comet's tails _____
   from the sun.

Explanation: Comets have solid centers, cloudy atmospheres called comas, and one or two tails. The direction a comet's tail flows is controlled by the sun. The tail of a comet is formed as it travels closer to the sun.

GRAVITY

Students will be pulled in to this Science in a Box *unit on gravity!*

Objective: to learn about the effects of gravity

Materials: class supply of Styrofoam cups and metal washers, 6 marbles, string or twine, sharpened pencil, permanent marker, ruler, scissors, large coffee can (39 oz. size works well), poster board, masking tape

Teacher preparation:
1. Follow the directions on page 3 to assemble your *Science in a Box* unit.
2. Place the items from the materials list above inside the shoebox, except the coffee can, poster board, and masking tape.
3. Make a gravity cone as follows: (1) On the poster board, draw a circle with a 22-inch diameter; (2) cut around the circle and then cut out a wedge that is one-eighth of the circle; (3) overlap the circle to form a cone that fits snugly in the coffee can with most of the cone sticking out of the top of the can (tape the cone so it does not open); and (4) tape the cone to the outside of the can.
4. On the day of the challenger activity, have the gravity cone available for students.

Background Information

Gravity is the force of attraction between two objects. The more *mass,* or amount of matter, a body has, the greater its gravitational pull. Were it not for the earth's velocity and the gravitational pull of the sun, the earth would move through space in a straight line. These two forces cause Earth to *orbit,* or travel around, the sun.

Answer Key for Student Activity

1. Earth would orbit the sun more quickly. Earth is closer to the sun, so it would complete its orbit faster.
2. The swinging cup makes a kind of artificial gravity, keeping the marbles at the bottom of the cup. The marbles represent everything on earth.

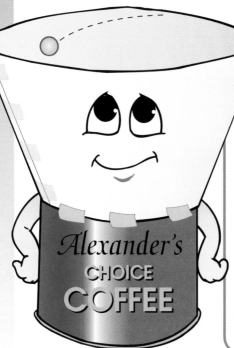

Fabulous Facts

Jupiter's gravitational pull is more than twice that of Earth's gravitational pull.

Every piece of matter in the universe, no matter how small, has gravitational force—even you!

Earth's ocean tides are a result of the gravitational pull of the sun and the moon.

Long before astronomer Percival Lowell could see Pluto, he predicted another planet existed beyond Neptune. He thought another planet's gravity was affecting the orbits of Neptune and Uranus.

EARTH

Gravity

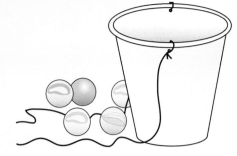

©The Education Center, Inc.

MATERIALS

class supply of
  Styrofoam cups
  and metal washers

6 marbles

string or twine

sharpened pencil

permanent marker

ruler

scissors

gravity cone

SAFETY RULES

1. Use all materials appropriately.

2. Make sure the string is securely tied to the washer.

3. Do not swing the string near people or other things.

4. Do not let go of the string while swinging it.

GRAVITY CHALLENGER

Objective: to understand that planets stay in orbit due to gravity
Materials: gravity cone, marble
Procedure:

1. Predict what will happen when you roll the marble around the inside top of the cone. Record your predictions on another sheet of paper or in your science notebook.
2. Roll the marble around the inside top of the cone as fast as possible, as shown, without it coming out of the cone. Observe its movement. Repeat two or three times.
3. Record how the marble moved. How is the marble's movement similar to a planet's orbit? How is it different?

Explanation: The funnel makes the marble move in a circular path while gravity pulls the marble downward. As the marble slows down, gravity forces the marble toward the bottom of the cone. Like the marble, Earth would crash into the sun if its forward speed decreased. The crash would be due to gravity being a greater force upon Earth than Earth's forward speed.

STUDENT ACTIVITY

GRAVITY

Purpose: to learn about the effects of gravity

Activity 1

A

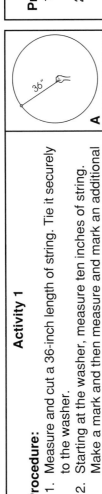

36"

B

18"

C

10"

Procedure:

1. Measure and cut a 36-inch length of string. Tie it securely to the washer.

2. Starting at the washer, measure ten inches of string. Make a mark and then measure and mark an additional 8 inches of string.

3. Look at illustrations A, B, and C. Which washer do you think will complete a circle the fastest? The slowest?

4. Try each experiment. At each length, swing the washer in a circle at your side. **Swing the washer only as hard as needed to keep the string taut.**

5. Were your predictions correct? _____ Explain.

Activity 2

Procedure:

1. Use the sharpened pencil to punch two holes under the rim and on opposite sides of the Styrofoam cup as shown.

2. Remove the washer (from Activity 1) and thread the string through the holes so that equal lengths of string are coming from each side.

3. Put six marbles into the cup. Hold the cup over the shoebox and tip the cup over. Observe how easily the marbles roll out. Predict what would happen to the marbles if the cup were swung upside down.

4. Put the marbles back in the cup, hold both ends of the string in one hand, and swing the cup in a circle at your side.

5. Was your prediction correct? _____ Explain.

Questions:

1. Using what you've learned about planets' orbits, would Jupiter or Earth orbit the sun more quickly? _____ Explain.

2. How is the cup in Activity 2 like the earth? _____

What do the marbles represent? _____

Explanation: The closer a planet is to the body around which it is orbiting, the stronger the gravitational pull on the planet. Therefore, since Mercury is closer to the sun, the gravitational pull on Mercury is stronger than the sun's pull on Earth. To stay in orbit, then, Mercury must travel at a greater velocity than Earth.
    To create a kind of artificial gravity in space, you would need to make a spinning space station—like a bicycle wheel. The floor would be the outside rim and the gravity's strength would depend on the speed of the spinning wheel. The faster the spin the stronger the gravity.

Note to the teacher: Use as directed on page 3.

135

RESOURCES

Looking for science resources? Try this Science in a Box
unit on the earth's resources!

Objective: to learn about renewable and nonrenewable resources

Materials: rock, piece of wood, small plant, picture of a fish, piece of coal, small bottle of oil, small bag of soil, class supply of small boxes (jewelry size) and chocolate candy, construction paper in assorted colors (including black and white), aluminum foil, tape, desk lamp with at least a 60-watt bulb

Teacher preparation:
1. Follow the directions on page 3 to assemble your *Science in a Box* unit.
2. Place the items from the materials list above inside the shoebox, except the small boxes and the lamp.
3. On the day of the challenger activity, place the small boxes and the lamp with the shoebox materials.

Background Information

Natural resources are divided into two categories: renewable and non-renewable. *Renewable resources* may be replaced by natural processes over time. Renewable resources can be living organisms, such as fish or a rain forest, or other materials that are affected by or used by living organisms, such as water and soil. *Nonrenewable resources* are nonliving materials in finite amounts that cannot be replaced or can only be replaced over extremely long periods of time, such as fossil fuels and minerals.

Answer Key for Student Activity
Chart:
nonrenewable—oil, soil, rock, coal
renewable—wood, plant, fish
Questions:
Responses will vary. Accept all reasonable responses.

Fabulous Facts

Oil and coal are nonrenewable resources that are almost 65 million years old!

Three-fourths of our energy today comes from non-renewable fossil fuels, while only about four percent comes from renewable resources, such as solar and wind energy.

Oil and gas reserves are only estimated to last about 40–70 more years.

About 125 years ago, about 90 percent of our energy came from wood—a renewable resource.

EARTH
Resources

MATERIALS

rock

piece of wood

small plant

picture of a fish

piece of coal

small bottle of oil

small bag of soil

class supply of
   small boxes and
   chocolate candy

construction paper
   in assorted colors

aluminum foil

tape

lamp

SAFETY RULES

1. Use all materials appropriately.

2. Be careful when touching the solar oven; it may become hot.

RESOURCES CHALLENGER

Objective: to learn about one renewable resource—solar energy

Materials: small box, construction paper in assorted colors, aluminum foil, tape, piece of chocolate candy, lamp

Procedure:

1. To create a solar oven, cover the inside of the box with either construction paper or aluminum foil. Then place the chocolate candy in the box. Place the box directly under the lamp and turn the lamp on to simulate solar energy. Keep track of the amount of time it takes to melt the candy.

2. Compare the amount of time it takes to melt your candy with your classmates' times. Which material melted the chocolate faster? Slower?

Explanation: Solar energy is a renewable resource. This means that it can be replaced as it is used. On another sheet of paper or in your science notebook, explain why certain materials absorb solar energy better than others. What are some of the problems with using solar energy?

Note to the teacher: Use as directed on page 3.

RESOURCES

Renewable resources are made naturally and can be replaced over time.

Nonrenewable resources can't be used again. Once they are used, they are gone forever or can only be replaced over extremely long periods of time.

Purpose: to learn about renewable and nonrenewable resources

Procedure:

1. Look at each object listed on the chart below.
2. Fill in the chart by putting an X in either the renewable or nonrenewable resource box for each object. In the last column, tell why you think the resource is renewable or nonrenewable.
3. Look around the room to find one product made from a renewable resource and one made from a nonrenewable resource. Write each item in the spaces provided on the chart. Complete the chart.

Object	Renewable	Nonrenewable	Explanation
rock			
wood			
plant			
fish			
coal			
oil			
soil			

Questions:

1. Was it easier to find renewable or nonrenewable resources around your classroom? _____

   Explain. _____

2. Do you think people should use more renewable resources or nonrenewable resources? _____

   Explain. _____

Explanation: Renewable resources, such as water or a rain forest, are constantly being renewed, restored, or replaced by natural processes over time. Nonrenewable resources, such as fossil fuels and minerals, are nonliving materials in limited amounts that cannot be replaced or can only be replaced over long periods of time. Nonrenewable resources could one day run out.

EARTH'S WATER SUPPLY

Make a real splash with this Science in a Box *unit on the earth's water supply!*

Objective: to learn about the earth's water supply

Materials: plastic gallon jug, salt, measuring spoons, ¼ cup measuring cup, 5 plastic cups, 2 colored plastic plates, blue food coloring, eyedropper, water, warm water

Teacher preparation:
1. Follow the directions on page 3 to assemble your *Science in a Box* unit.
2. Use a permanent marker to label each of two plates *salt water* and *freshwater* and each of three cups with the letters *A, B,* and *C*.
3. Place the cups, plates, and the items from the materials list above inside the shoebox, except the water.
4. On the day of the student activity, have water available for students.
5. On the day of the challenger activity, have warm water available for students.

Background Information

If you look at Earth from space, it's obvious that about 70 percent of the planet is covered with water. The water in the oceans is salt water—the same salt you use on your food! But because humans need freshwater, we can't drink anything that comes right from the oceans. Freshwater is found in rivers, in lakes, underground, and frozen solid in the polar ice caps and glaciers. Almost all the water that we use on a daily basis comes from underground sources that we call groundwater.

Answer Key for Student Activity

lakes and rivers: Cup C
oceans: Jug
groundwater: Cup B
polar ice caps and glaciers: Cup A
Questions:
Responses will vary. Accept all reasonable responses.

Fabulous Facts

One quart of used motor oil is capable of polluting up to one million gallons of groundwater!

Only about half of all the water in underground sources can be brought to the surface. The rest is buried too deep to retrieve.

Scientists think that if all the groundwater in North America could be brought to the surface, it could cover the continent with a sheet of water almost 100 feet thick!

EARTH
Earth's Water Supply

©The Education Center, Inc.

MATERIALS

plastic gallon jug

salt

measuring spoons

¼ cup measuring cup

5 plastic cups

2 colored plastic plates

blue food coloring

eyedropper

water

warm water

SAFETY RULES

1. Use all materials appropriately.

2. Do not drink the water used in the experiments.

EARTH'S WATER SUPPLY CHALLENGER

Objective: to learn about one difference between salt water and freshwater
Materials: salt, measuring spoons, 2 plastic cups, 2 colored plastic plates, eyedropper, warm water
Procedure:

1. Pour ¼ cup of warm water into a cup. Add one tablespoon of salt and stir until the salt has dissolved.
2. Pour ¼ cup of warm water in a second cup.
3. Use the eyedropper to place several drops of freshwater and salt water on the appropriate plates. Set them in a warm dry place to allow the water to evaporate.
4. On another sheet of paper or in your science notebook, predict what you will see when the water has evaporated. Once the water has evaporated, record the results. Was your prediction correct? Explain.
5. Rinse and dry the plates so they are clean for the next group.

Explanation: About 70 percent of the earth is covered with water. The water in the oceans is salt water, containing dissolved sodium chloride—the same salt you use on your food! But because humans need freshwater, we can't drink anything that comes right from the oceans. When salt water has evaporated, the salt is left behind.

©The Education Center, Inc. • *Science in a Box* • TEC1749

EARTH'S WATER SUPPLY

Purpose: to learn how much of the water on Earth is freshwater

Procedure:

1. Fill a one-gallon jug with water. Add several drops of blue food coloring. Cap the jug and gently shake it until the water appears blue. (This water represents all of the water on Earth.)

2. Using the water from the jug and measuring spoons, measure and pour the following amounts into each cup:
   Cup A: 5½ tablespoons
   Cup B: 1½ tablespoons
   Cup C: ⅛ teaspoon

3. Predict what water sources the remaining water in the jug and the water in each cup represent. Write the letter of the cup or the word *jug* in the spaces provided.

   lakes and rivers _____

   oceans _____

   groundwater _____

   polar ice caps and glaciers _____

4. Read the following information.

Ocean water makes up about 97.2% of all the earth's water. Polar ice caps and glaciers make up about 2.11%. Groundwater makes up about .62%. Lakes and rivers make up about .091% of all the earth's water.

Questions:

1. Based on the information in the box, was your prediction correct? _____

2. Are you surprised by the amount of water in each category? _____ Which amount surprises you the most?
   _____ Why? _____

   _____

   _____

3. Why do you think it is important to protect our freshwater supply? _____

   _____

   _____

Explanation: Although the oceans cover about 70 percent of the earth's surface, they are unusable sources for drinking, industry, or agriculture. Only about three percent of the water on Earth is freshwater. Of this three percent, only about one-third of one percent is available for human use.

SOIL

Dig into your science lesson with this Science in a Box
unit on soil!

Objective: to learn about the properties of soil

Materials: 1 cup each of topsoil and potting soil per student, 2 cups of schoolyard soil per student, 3 clear plastic cups, 2 Styrofoam cups, three 1" square cotton gauze pads per student, plastic spoon, eyedropper, magnifying glass, white paper, colander, mesh strainer, water, toothpicks

Teacher preparation:
1. Follow the directions on page 3 to assemble your *Science in a Box* unit.
2. Place the items from the materials list above inside the shoebox, except the soil, the collander, the strainer, and the water.
3. On the day of the student activity, students will need all three types of soil and access to water.
4. On the day of the challenger activity, each student will need the collander, the strainer, and about one cup of schoolyard soil.

Background Information

Soil covers most of our land and is crucial in sustaining life. Soil holds roots, stores nutrients, and contains the decomposition of dead plants and animals. Most soil is made up of minerals (45%); water (25%); air (25%); and *humus,* or organic material from dead plants and animals (5%). Some of the minerals in soil are made up of small gravel or rock, sand, silt, and clay. The size and nature of these particles in each soil sample determine how likely the soil is to hold water. The ability to hold water has a great effect on how a plant will be able to sustain growth.

Answer Key for Student Activity

Responses will vary. Possible responses:
Chart:
potting soil—about 161 drops of water
topsoil—about 153 drops of water
schoolyard soil—about 305 drops of
  water
Questions:
1. rocks, twigs, clay, clumps of soil, grass, tree bark
2. topsoil
3. topsoil
4. schoolyard soil
5. Responses will vary. Accept all reasonable responses.

Fabulous Facts

There are over 70,000 different types of soil in the United States alone!

Dark soils are usually better plant growers than light soils because of the larger amount of humus.

Since 1935, the FBI has collected and studied soil samples for use in thousands of criminal investigations a year.

It can take nature over 500 years to make one inch of topsoil!

One acre of soil can sustain 10,000 to 20,000 pounds of animal life!

EARTH

Soil

MATERIALS

- 1 cup each of topsoil and potting soil per student
- 2 cups of schoolyard soil per student
- 3 clear plastic cups
- 2 Styrofoam cups
- three 1" square cotton gauze pads per student
- plastic spoon

- eyedropper
- magnifying glass
- white paper
- colander
- mesh strainer
- water
- toothpicks

SAFETY RULES

1. Wash your hands before and after touching the soil samples.

2. Use all materials appropriately.

SOIL CHALLENGER

Objective: to learn about the different elements of soil

Materials: 1 cup of schoolyard soil, 3 clear plastic cups, white paper, colander, mesh strainer

Procedure:

1. Lay the paper on your desk or table. Place the colander on the paper and pour the schoolyard soil into it. Shake the colander over the paper until no fragments fall through.

2. Put the fragments left in the colander into a clear plastic cup. Pour the remaining fragments from the paper into the strainer. Shake the strainer over the paper until no fragments fall through. Put the fragments left in the strainer into a cup. Put the fragments left on the paper into the remaining cup. What do you notice about the fragments in the three cups?

3. On another sheet of paper or in your science notebook, record your observations. What does soil consist of? Are you surprised by what you see? Explain.

Explanation: Soil is made up of varying sizes of minerals such as rocks, sand, silt, and clay. It also has air, water, and traces of *humus,* or dead plants and animals.

Note to the teacher: Use as directed on page 3.

STUDENT ACTIVITY

SOIL

Purpose: to learn about the properties of soil

Activity 1: Soil Examination
Procedure:
1. Using a plastic spoon, take a small amount of soil from each container and place it in separate piles on a white sheet of paper.
2. Use a magnifying glass to examine the soil.
3. Complete the chart below.

How the soil...	potting soil	topsoil	schoolyard soil
looks			
feels			
smells			

Activity 2: Water Retainability
Procedure:
1. Using a toothpick, carefully poke a hole in the bottom of a Styrofoam cup.
2. Place a gauze pad in the bottom of the cup, covering the hole. Add three spoonfuls of the first soil sample. On the chart below, predict how many water drops it will take before the water begins to leak.
3. Hold another cup under the cup with the soil to catch the water as it drains. Use the eyedropper to add water to the soil one drop at a time to find out whether your prediction is correct. Record your information on the chart. Repeat Steps 2–3 with the remaining soil samples.

	potting soil	topsoil	schoolyard soil
Predicted number of water drops			
Actual number of water drops			

Questions:
1. When examining the soil samples, what did you observe? _____
2. Which soil is the darkest? _____
3. Through which soil did the water drain the fastest? _____
4. Which soil held the most water? _____
5. Which soil would you want to use to grow a vegetable garden? _____ Why? _____

Explanation: Plants need to absorb water from the soil through their roots. Soil is made up of minerals such as rocks, sand, silt, and clay. It also has air, water, and traces of *humus*, or dead plants and animals. These factors help the soil hold the right amount of water for different types of plants to grow.

Note to the teacher: Use as directed on page 3.

EROSION AND WEATHERING

Your science lesson won't get washed away with this Science in a Box *unit on erosion and weathering!*

Objective: to learn about slow changes on the earth's surface

Materials: 4 types of soil (topsoil, potting soil, sand and soil mixture, rock and soil mixture), baking sheet, 1-cup measuring cup, class supply of ice cubes, various rocks (some containing limestone), chalk, vinegar, clear plastic cup

Teacher preparation:
1. Follow the directions on page 3 to assemble your *Science in a Box* unit.
2. Place the items from the materials list above inside the shoebox, except the ice.
3. Before the day of the student activity, make a class supply of "glaciers." Put twigs and/or rocks in ice cube trays and then add water. Freeze overnight.
4. On the day of the student activity, students will need access to the "glaciers."

Background Information

The earth's surface is constantly attacked by forces that break up and carry away soil and rocks. *Weathering* is the wearing down of rocks by water, wind, and other means. *Erosion* is the carrying away of weathered rocks. These processes are continuous but are generally slow and can take millions of years to change the earth's surface. Moving water in rivers, waves, and glaciers is the greatest force changing the earth's surface. Wind, constant heating and cooling, and plant growth are also factors that break up and move rocks.

Answer Key for Student Activity

1. The glacier caused twigs and rocks to move to the sides while it pushed the soil and small items in front of it.
2. The glacier left valleys and streaks of rock and soil.
3. A pile of soil, rocks, and twigs was left in the glacier's place.

Fabulous Facts

Scientists estimate that the rate of dissolving limestone is only about $1/20$ of a centimeter in 100 years! It would take 60 million years to dissolve 300 meters of limestone in this way!

Weathering can affect rocks as far as 600 feet below the surface!

Since Columbus sailed to North America, the Atlantic Ocean has gotten about 33 feet wider because of the slow process of seafloor spreading.

EARTH
Erosion and Weathering

©The Education Center, Inc.

MATERIALS

4 types of soil (top-soil, potting soil, sand and soil mixture, rock and soil mixture)

baking sheet

1-cup measuring cup

class supply of "glaciers"

various rocks (some containing limestone)

chalk

vinegar

clear plastic cup

SAFETY RULES

1. Use all materials appropriately.

2. Do not eat the ice used in the student activity.

EROSION AND WEATHERING CHALLENGER

Objective: to learn about acid rain
Materials: various rocks, chalk, vinegar, clear plastic cup
Procedure:

1. Place the rocks and chalk in the cup so that they are not touching. (You may have to test them separately if they are too big to be tested together.) Pour vinegar over them so they are covered.

2. What is happening to the rocks? The chalk? On another sheet of paper or in your science notebook, record your observations.

Explanation: One type of slow change that affects the earth's surface is *weathering,* or the process of rocks breaking into smaller pieces. One type of weathering is caused by a chemical change. Acid rain can cause a chemical change in carbonate rocks, such as limestone. Chalk is a type of limestone. Explain how the vinegar in the experiment is like acid rain. Although it takes about 100 years to dissolve $1/20$ of a centimeter of limestone, how might weathering affect buildings made of limestone?

©The Education Center, Inc. • *Science in a Box* • TEC1749

EROSION AND WEATHERING

Purpose: to learn how glaciers cause erosion

Procedure:

1. Place one cup of each type of soil on a baking sheet so that they touch but do not get mixed together as shown. Smooth the soils.
2. Predict what would happen to each type of soil if a glacier were to move through it. Record your predictions on the chart below.

3. Test your predictions by taking an ice cube (glacier) and placing it on one of the soils. Slowly push it through the soil, applying pressure. (Do not press down so hard that you can see the bottom of the baking sheet.) Record your observations on the chart.
4. Repeat Step 3 for each soil type.

Predictions and observations:

Soil Type	Prediction	Result
topsoil (has small sticks)		
rocky soil		
sandy soil		
potting soil		

Questions:

1. What did the "glacier" do to the soil as it moved through it? _____

_____

2. How did the "glacier" change the surface of the soil? _____

_____

3. When you stopped pushing the "glacier" and removed it, what was left in the glacier's place? _____

_____

Explanation: Glaciers cause erosion on the earth's surface as they move. This is due to the weight of the ice and the particles carried by the ice. Glaciers leave behind valleys, peaks, ridges, cliffs, lakes, piles of rocks, and huge boulders. Glaciers also carry away tons of sediment and redeposit it in other locations.

RAPID SURFACE CHANGES

Shake, rattle, and flow with this Science in a Box
unit on rapid surface changes!

Objective: to learn about rapid surface changes

Materials: 20 oz. plastic soda bottle, liquid measuring cup, tablespoon measure, baking soda, sheet of construction paper, dishwashing liquid, red food coloring, vinegar, 2 rectangular boards (approximately 1" x 4" x 6"), stick of modeling clay, 2 Monopoly houses, 2 Monopoly hotels, toothpicks, cookie sheet, reference materials on volcanoes

Teacher preparation:
1. Follow the directions on page 3 to assemble your *Science in a Box* unit.
2. Place the items from the materials list above inside the shoebox, except the cookie sheet and the reference materials.
3. On the day of the challenger activity, have the cookie sheet and reference materials available for students.

Fabulous Facts

There are about 35 earthquakes every day in the United States! There are over one million earthquakes each year throughout the world!

The word *volcano* is borrowed from the Roman god Vulcan, who was the god of fire. He was said to live on a tiny island off the coast of Sicily that was named Vulcano.

The energy released in one earthquake in 1964 had the same amount of energy as 73,000 early atomic bombs!

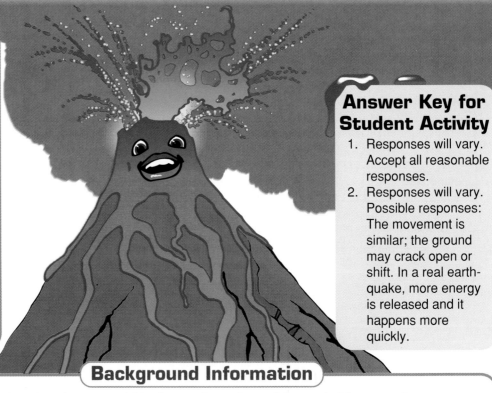

Answer Key for Student Activity

1. Responses will vary. Accept all reasonable responses.
2. Responses will vary. Possible responses: The movement is similar; the ground may crack open or shift. In a real earthquake, more energy is released and it happens more quickly.

Background Information

Volcanoes and earthquakes can quickly change the surface of the earth. They are often very powerful forces and can cause an area's destruction. Volcanoes can also cause an area's rebirth. These powerful, rapid surface changes, however, are largely due to very slow changes beneath the surface. Scientists believe that continents sit on slowly moving plates in the earth's crust and upper mantle. It is at the edges of these plates that most volcanic and seismic activity occurs. The plates are constantly pushing over and under, moving away from, or sliding alongside one another. These plate movements have made volcanoes, earthquakes, and mountains.

EARTH
Rapid Surface Changes

©The Education Center, Inc.

MATERIALS

- 20 oz. plastic soda bottle
- liquid measuring cup
- tablespoon measure
- baking soda
- sheet of construction paper
- dishwashing liquid
- red food coloring
- vinegar
- 2 rectangular boards (approximately 1" x 4" x 6")
- stick of modeling clay
- 2 Monopoly houses
- 2 Monopoly hotels
- toothpicks
- cookie sheet
- reference materials on volcanoes

SAFETY RULES

1. Use all materials appropriately.

2. Be careful of splinters when working with wood.

RAPID SURFACE CHANGES CHALLENGER

Objective: to make a model of a volcanic eruption

Materials: cookie sheet, 20 oz. plastic soda bottle, liquid measuring cup, tablespoon measure, baking soda, sheet of construction paper, dishwashing liquid, red food coloring, vinegar, reference materials on volcanoes

Procedure:
1. Put the empty bottle in the center of the cookie sheet.
2. Make a funnel from the construction paper.
3. Using the measuring spoon and the funnel, put four tablespoons of baking soda into the bottle. Remove the funnel.
4. Add 1/2 tablespoon dishwashing liquid and ten drops of red food coloring.
5. Predict what will happen when you add the vinegar. Record your prediction on another sheet of paper or in your science notebook.
6. Pour 1/2 cup vinegar into the bottle, and observe your volcano. Record what happens.
7. Research to find which type of volcano is shaped most like the bottle and which type erupts as in the experiment.

Explanation: When Earth's heat melts rock, it forms magma and produces gases. The magma-gas mixture is lighter than solid rock and slowly rises toward Earth's surface. Eventually it causes a chamber to form near the surface. Meanwhile, the surrounding rock exerts a great deal of pressure on the magma chamber, and the magma moves upward, melting a path through the weakest part of the rock. If the magma reaches the surface, the gas and magma is released—sometimes explosively. At this point the magma becomes lava. In what ways is your model similar to and different from a real volcano?

©The Education Center, Inc. • *Science in a Box* • TEC1749

RAPID SURFACE CHANGES

Purpose: to learn about earthquakes and their effects

Movement Along Faults

Normal Fault	Reverse Fault	Strike-Slip Fault
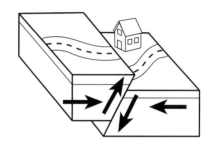		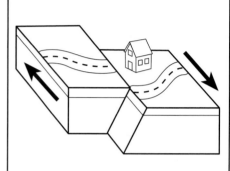
Plates are pulling apart as one plate moves up and the other moves down.	Plates are pushing together as one plate pushes under the other.	Plates are moving past one another along the fault.

Procedure:

1. Set up the boards (plates), clay (surface), toothpicks (road), and buildings similar to the illustration. (The clay should be about $1/8$-inch thick.)
2. Predict how the surface (clay) will be affected by each of the fault movements shown above. Record your predictions on another sheet of paper or in your science notebook.
3. Place one board in each hand, holding the clay in place. Slowly move the boards in the direction shown by the arrows in the first box above. What happened to the surface? The buildings? The road? Record your observations.
4. Reset the clay, buildings, and toothpicks.
5. Repeat Steps 3 and 4 to test each of the fault movements shown.

Questions

1. Which fault caused the most change to the position of the buildings? _____

_____ The road?_____

2. How is this model similar to or different from what occurs with an actual earthquake? _____

_____

_____

Explanation: An earthquake occurs when the plates along a *fault,* or the space between two plates, suddenly slip. As the plates push together, pull apart, or slide past each other, pressure builds and eventually slips. The released energy from this slipping then travels in the form of waves through the ground, resulting in an earthquake.

WEATHER

Nothing but clear skies ahead with this Science in a Box
unit on weather!

Objective: to learn about two predictors of weather

Materials: clear bowl, red and blue food coloring, empty film canister, red and blue crayons, 5 index cards per student, reference materials on clouds, warm and cold water

Teacher preparation:
1. Follow the directions on page 3 to assemble your *Science in a Box* unit.
2. Place the items from the materials list above inside the shoebox, except the water and reference materials.
3. On the day of the student activity, have warm and cold water available for students.
4. On the day of the challenger activity, have reference materials on clouds available for students.

Background Information

Meteorologists use data from measurements taken throughout the day to predict the development and movement of weather systems. They use various weather instruments to monitor the atmosphere, such as an *electronic thermometer* (registers the highest and lowest temperatures of the day), *hygrometer* (measures water vapor in the air), *barometer* (measures air pressure), *weather vane* (shows wind direction), and *rain gauge* (measures rainfall or snowfall). Clouds can also provide reliable clues about forecasting weather.

Answer Key for Student Activity

1. The cold blue water mixed with the cold water. The warm red water stayed on top of the cold water.
2. Cold air is heavier than warm air, so it sinks. Warm air is lighter than cold air, so it rises.

Fabulous Facts

Our modern weather balloons are modeled after a hot-air balloon invented by the French Montgolfier brothers in 1783.

In 1972 an unmanned weather balloon reached a record altitude of 170,000 feet!

Cloud study and classification began in 1803 by Luke Howard, a British meteorologist.

Clouds that can only be seen in high altitudes are known as "mother-of-pearl" clouds.

EARTH

Weather

MATERIALS

clear bowl

red and blue food coloring

empty film canister

red and blue crayons

5 index cards per student

reference materials on clouds

warm and cold water

SAFETY RULES

1. Use all materials appropriately.

2. Do not drink the water used in the student activity.

WEATHER CHALLENGER

Objective: to learn about cloud types and what type of weather they help to predict

Materials: 5 index cards, reference materials on clouds

Procedure:

1. Research each cloud type listed in Box A to find its Latin meaning, what it looks like, and at least two additional facts. On one side of an index card, write the name and draw a picture of each cloud. On the back of the corresponding card, record each cloud's Latin meaning and the researched facts.

2. Research to find the definitions of *alto* and *nimbus.* Record each word and its definition on separate index cards.

3. Use the cards to figure out the meanings of the clouds listed in Box B and also what type of weather they may bring. On another sheet of paper or in your science notebook, record the name of each cloud and the information.

Explanation: Knowing about the different types of clouds can help predict what type of weather will be in an area. Each type of cloud may signify that a particular type of weather is on the way.

Box A
cumulus
stratus
cirrus

Box B
cumulonimbus
cirrostratus
cirrocumulus
nimbostratus
stratocumulus
altostratus
altocumulus

WEATHER

Purpose: to learn about warm and cold air patterns and what type of weather they help to predict

Procedure:
1. Fill the bowl about three-fourths full with cold water.
2. Place one drop of blue food coloring in the empty film canister; then fill it with cold water.
3. Holding the canister upright, slowly lower it to the bottom of the bowl.
4. Observe what happens to the blue water (cold air). Draw a picture of the results in the first box below.
5. Take the canister out of the bowl and dump the water out of both. Repeat Steps 1–3 except place red food coloring and warm water in the canister. Observe what happens to the red water (warm air). Draw a picture of the results in the second box below.

Questions:

1. Describe the differences you saw in how the two colored waters reacted to the cold water. _____

_____

2. What conclusions can you draw about how cold air and warm air react when they come in contact with each other?

_____

_____

Explanation: Uneven heating of the earth's surface causes the air to be in constant motion. Warm air is lighter than cold air. As cold air sinks, it causes warm air to rise. The horizontal movement of air is called wind. Because large parts of the earth's atmosphere are heated unevenly, global, or *prevailing,* winds blow constantly. Most weather systems in the United States move from west to east due to prevailing winds. Understanding wind helps predict what type of weather an area may have.

SCIENCE IN A BOX
Objective Index

Page Number	Unit Title	Student Activity Objectives	Challenger Objectives
4	**Matter**	identify the properties of matter in three states	identify the state of matter of a mixture
8	**States of Water**	observe the changing states of water	observe the effects of heat energy on states of matter
12	**Force and Motion**	observe Newton's laws of motion with everyday objects	show how force applied to objects affects their motion and how motion is related to the strength of the force applied
16	**Inertia**	learn about the law of inertia	observe an object remaining at rest as a result of inertia
20	**Reflection**	learn about light reflection by testing various surfaces	make a surface that reflects an image
24	**Refraction**	learn about refraction and how it works	learn about refraction through a prism
28	**Sound**	learn that sound is caused by vibrations	find out whether sound can travel through a solid
32	**Pitch**	learn about pitch	identify levels of pitch
36	**Transmitting Heat**	learn about the predictable movement of heat	find out whether an object's temperature will rise as its state changes
40	**Simple Circuits**	learn about simple circuits using a bulb, a battery, and wires	make a simple circuit and short circuit
44	**Parallel and Series Circuits**	learn about parallel and series circuits using bulbs, batteries, and wires	learn about parallel and series circuit setups for batteries
48	**Electromagnets**	make an electromagnet	determine which materials can be magnetized by electricity
52	**Magnetic Poles**	discover that all magnets have two poles and that poles attract and repel	examine the repelling power of magnets
56	**Plant and Animal Cells**	learn the similarities and differences of plant and animal cells	learn about the cell membrane
60	**Systems**	learn that a system is a collection of parts working together to perform a function	understand the impact of climatic systems on plant and animal life
64	**Adaptations**	learn about bird beak adaptations	determine how a bird adapts its feeding strategy when its environment abruptly changes
68	**Plant Life Cycles**	learn that seeds have the basic parts needed to grow into a plant	learn about the life cycle of a plant
72	**Animal Life Cycles**	learn about animal life cycles	learn about three factors in an animal's life cycle
76	**Behavior**	learn how external stimuli can affect an organism's behavior	learn the effect of external stimuli on behavior
80	**Inherited Characteristics**	learn about inherited characteristics	identify inherited characteristics
84	**Extinction**	imagine what animals might do to survive as their habitats change	show how an animal's range changes as its numbers decrease
88	**Vertebrates and Invertebrates**	learn about vertebrates and invertebrates	compare the human backbone with the backbone of other vertebrates and the physical support systems of invertebrates
92	**Circulatory System**	learn about the blood	learn about how the heart beats at different rates
96	**Digestive System**	learn about the human digestive system and how it works	learn about how the small intestine works
100	**Respiratory System**	understand how the lungs and diaphragm work together	observe lung capacity
104	**Nervous System**	learn about the nervous system and how it works	learn how the nervous system and the senses work together
108	**Water Cycle**	show how water infiltration and surface runoff play their parts in the water cycle	demonstrate the water cycle
112	**Rocks**	learn about the different characteristics of rocks	learn about sedimentary and metamorphic rocks
116	**Layers of the Earth**	learn about the layers of the earth	learn about how the crust is made up of plates
120	**Fossils**	better understand amber fossils	understand how paleontologists remove fossils from rocks
124	**The Sun's Energy**	learn about the sun as a heat source	learn why some areas of the earth receive more heat and light than other areas
128	**Comets**	learn about comets	learn how comets decrease in size
132	**Gravity**	learn about the effects of gravity	understand that planets stay in orbit due to gravity
136	**Resources**	learn about renewable and nonrenewable resources	learn about one renewable resource—solar energy
140	**Earth's Water Supply**	learn how much of the water on Earth is freshwater	learn about one difference between saltwater and freshwater
144	**Soil**	learn about the properties of soil	learn about the different elements of soil
148	**Erosion and Weathering**	learn how glaciers cause erosion	learn about acid rain
152	**Rapid Surface Changes**	learn about earthquakes and their effects	make a model of a volcanic eruption
156	**Weather**	learn about warm and cold air patterns and what type of weather they help predict	learn about cloud types and what type of weather they help predict